WHERE HAVE ALL THE PROPHETS GONE?

WHERE HAVE ALL THE PROPHETS GONE?

Reclaiming Prophetic
Preaching in America

Marvin A. McMickle

THE PILGRIM PRESS  CLEVELAND

The Pilgrim Press, 700 Prospect Avenue, Cleveland, Ohio 44115,
thepilgrimpress.com

Biblical quotations are from the New Revised Standard Version of
the Bible, © 1989 by the Division of Christian Education of the
National Council of the Churches of Christ in the U.S.A., and are
used by permission. Some changes have been made for inclusivity.

This book has been reproduced as a digital reprint.

Library of Congress Cataloging-in-Publication Data

McMickle, Marvin A.
    Where have all the prophets gone? : reclaiming prophetic
preaching in America / Marvin A. McMickle.
        p. cm.
    Includes bibliographical references.
    ISBN-13: 978-0-8298-1720-1
    1. Preaching.   I. Title.
    BV4211.3.M39   2006
    251—dc22   2006025637

    ISBN-13 : 978-0-8298-1837-6 (paperback)

WHERE HAVE ALL THE PROPHETS GONE?

Reclaiming Prophetic
Preaching in America

Marvin A. McMickle

THE PILGRIM PRESS  CLEVELAND

The Pilgrim Press, 700 Prospect Avenue, Cleveland, Ohio 44115, thepilgrimpress.com

Biblical quotations are from the New Revised Standard Version of the Bible, © 1989 by the Division of Christian Education of the National Council of the Churches of Christ in the U.S.A., and are used by permission. Some changes have been made for inclusivity.

This book has been reproduced as a digital reprint.

Library of Congress Cataloging-in-Publication Data

McMickle, Marvin A.
    Where have all the prophets gone? : reclaiming prophetic preaching in America / Marvin A. McMickle.
        p. cm.
    Includes bibliographical references.
    ISBN-13: 978-0-8298-1720-1
    1. Preaching.   I. Title.
    BV4211.3.M39   2006
    251—dc22   2006025637

    ISBN-13 : 978-0-8298-1837-6 (paperback)

Contents

PREFACE
AND
ACKNOWLEDGMENTS

This book is intended to raise one specific challenge: the need to restore prophetic preaching to a place of urgency in the life of the American church. This book then takes on the challenge of identifying those forces and false practices that have obscured or replaced prophetic preaching in so many churches. Four such obstructions will be named and discussed: a narrow definition of justice that does not extend beyond abortion and same-sex marriage, the emergence of an oxymoron called patriot pastors, the focus on praise and worship that does not result in any duty and discipleship, and, finally, the vile messages of prosperity theology that seem to have overtaken the pulpits and the airwaves used by televangelists across this country.

What makes the need for prophetic preaching so urgent are the issues confronting this nation about which America's pulpits should be thundering a message of godly concern and criticism of both our political leadership and the body politic as a whole. Instead, too many preachers in this country content themselves with the issues listed above. Nothing is said about the human, emotional, and financial costs of the war in Iraq. Nothing is said about the costs and consequences of having over two million persons packed into our nation's overcrowded prisons, most of them for drug-related offenses that could be treated more effectively and with much less expense without incarceration. There are forty-five million persons in this country who have no medical insurance. Racism and sexism continue to rage throughout this country, and that is as true in the church as it is in the general public.

The church of Jesus Christ must be challenged about these and other urgent matters that confront our society. This book is a challenge to those who occupy the nation's pulpits to rise above those topics that seem so popular these days, and lay claim to the prophetic tradition of the Bible. It is not too late to preach a prophetic word to a sinful world, and such preaching cannot begin too soon! There are preachers across the country that never laid down the mantle of prophetic preaching; blessings on each one of them. This is a call for others to join their ranks.

ACKNOWLEDGMENTS

I want to express my thanks and appreciation to the many people who helped to shape and refine the arguments that are found within this book. The first audience was the Academy of Homiletics, before whom the basic hypothesis of the book was shared as a paper during our meeting in Memphis, Tennessee, in 2004. The second audience involved the readers of *The African American Pulpit,* where the academy paper was reprinted and because of which much needed feedback was provided. The third audience was a workshop group at the Samuel Dewitt Proctor Black Church Leadership Institute that met in Jacksonville, Florida, in 2005. Finally, I also had the chance to share some of this material with colleagues who gathered at Bethany Baptist Church in Brooklyn, New York, in September 2005 for the first annual William Augustus Jones Jr. Preaching Institute.

Peer review is an invaluable aspect of the writing enterprise, and my peers and colleagues did not let our friendship stand in the way of their objective assessment of the material found in this book. The improvements that have occurred since the paper was first presented in December 2004 are to be credited to them. The shortcomings that remain in terms of too much overgeneralization or hyperbole should all be credited to me.

I am indebted to Kim Sadler and Kris Firth at The Pilgrim Press for their expertise in helping me transform my material into this finished product. Both of them were careful and critical readers who made wonderful suggestions as to the ways by which the book could be helpful to a wider audience of readers. I am also grateful to them for their patience as I pushed the deadlines for completing the final manuscript to the very limit.

Finally I am indebted to two people in particular. Theirs may have been the most important contributions of all. One of them is a woman I met at Lakeside Association, a United Methodist owned summer camp and retreat center on the shores of Lake Erie in Ohio. I did a brief discussion of this forthcoming book with a group of persons who gathered for a luncheon while I was serving as chaplain for the week in August 2006. She reminded me that she proudly referred to herself as a conservative, evangelical Christian who did not fit into any of the categories and who did not conform to any of the ideologies or political views that the news media assigns to that part of the body of Christ. It should be stated that when I refer to conservative, evangelical Christians throughout this book, it is the group that is so frequently in the news media for their political views that I have in mind, not this saintly soul and others like her who lend honor to the term conservative, evangelical Christians.

The other person I must thank publicly is the Rev. Dr. Jeremiah Wright, senior pastor of Trinity United Church of Christ in Chicago, Illinois. All who read this book will see his warm and generous endorsement of its contents. I am grateful to him for the things he has written publicly. However, I am even more grateful to him for the private comments he made about not overlooking the many areas in which the mainline Protestant community is involved in the work of justice well beyond the ways that seem to capture the attention of the news media. I am certain that those who read this book will want to say that both the comments from the woman from Lakeside and from Dr. Wright should have been taken even more to heart. I am indebted to both of them.

ONE

WHAT IS
PROPHETIC PREACHING AND
WHY IS IT IMPORTANT?

But now, thus says God . . .

—Isaiah 43:1

O ne of the essential needs in every congregation of believers is an occasional sermon rooted in the words
and witness of the Old Testament prophets. Preachers
need to play a role within the life of their congregation
and their community similar to the role that such people
as Amos, Jeremiah, and Micah played within the life of
the nations of Israel and Judah. James Ward and Christine
Ward begin their important book on this subject of
prophetic preaching by writing:

> The natural inclination of the Christian commu-
> nity, like all religious communities, is to adapt its
> witness of faith to its most immediate human
> needs. In doing this the community always runs
> the risk of obscuring the wider dimensions of the
> gospel, particularly the wider implications of

God's demand for righteousness and justice. What is needed, therefore, is preaching that recovers these wider dimensions and illuminates the ways in which the community obscures them.[1]

Those who preach must appreciate the need to let their sermons play this role in the life of their church, their surrounding community, and the wider society in which the preacher is a member.

Within congregational life, there is a tendency for the preacher to become preoccupied with such pressing matters as new members' or confirmation classes; the maintenance or renovation of the church building; whether or not the annual budget will be met; and how to maintain a feeling of intimacy in the face of a rapidly growing or shifting membership. What may be lost in the rush to respond to these issues is that congregation's responsibility to respond to an escalating problem of homelessness in the community, or overcrowding in the jails, or the abuse of drugs and alcohol by youngsters in the local school district. It is the preacher's job to remain watchful, to use the image of Ezekiel 3 and 33, and to sound the alarm about the injuries that are being inflicted upon people as well as about the injustices that are taking place.

THE FUNCTION OF PROPHETIC PREACHING

Prophetic preaching shifts the focus of a congregation from what is happening to them as a local church to what is happening to them as a part of society. Prophetic preaching then asks the question, "What is the role or the appropriate response of our congregation, our association, and our denomination to the events that are occurring within our society and throughout the world?" Prophetic preaching points out those false gods of comfort. Further, it points out a lack of concern and acquiescence in the face of evil that can so easily replace the true God of scripture who calls true believers to the active pursuit of justice and righteousness for every member of society. Prophetic preaching also never allows the community of faith to believe that participation in the rituals of religious life can ever be an adequate substitute for that form of ministry that is designed to uplift the "least of these" in our world.

The words of Amos and Micah, the eighth century B.C.E. prophets come immediately to mind. Both of them condemned Israel because that nation seemed more interested in the acts of animal sacrifice and the observance of religious feast days than in the poverty and economic exploitation that impacted the lives of so many people in their society. The voices of the biblical prophets echoed from the top of Mt. Carmel where Elijah confronted Ahab, Jezebel, and the priests of Baal to the streets of Jerusalem where John the Baptist challenged Herod Antipas.

The prophets preached truth to power, attacking the monarchs and the ruling elite for putting more confidence in armies and alliances than they did in the God who had brought them into that land. The prophets challenged the people of Israel who believed that God would never abandon them no matter how far the nation strayed from the covenant it had established with God at Sinai. With an urgency that could not be contained and a fervor that could not be controlled, the prophets declared, "Thus says God," despite the ridicule, rebuke, and outright rejection that most of them experienced throughout their lives. It is impossible to imagine the biblical narrative being told without the pronouncements of the prophets.

THE NEED FOR PROPHETIC PREACHING

As preaching schedules are being planned and as biblical texts and topics are being considered, it is easy to see the need for prophetic preaching in our churches and throughout our society. Many Christians worship in immaculately maintained churches that are situated in neighborhoods that look like bombed out war zones. Many Christians drive from the suburbs to churches located within a community that has been ravaged by poverty, drug trafficking, the loss of industry through outsourcing and factory closings, and underfunded and overwhelmed public school systems. Of course, on the other hand, many Christians never have to see these sights or confront the people and problems in these inner city communities. They have selected to move out of the inner city to pristine outer ring suburbs and have also moved their churches to those upscale areas.

For those who continue to travel into the crumbling and decaying cities of our nation, it is crucial that they hear a prophetic word about the problems that surround their church, the social policies that are the root cause of those problems, and what they can do as an expression of their biblical faith to bring about change. For those who live and worship in exurbia and who never get close enough to the grimy side of America for anything to rub off on them, prophetic preaching becomes even more urgent. It is crucial that people with wealth, power, and influence be challenged by a prophetic word that calls upon them to direct their resources not simply for tax advantages for themselves, but for a fairer and more just society for their fellow citizens.

The benefit of a regular use of materials taken from prophetic texts is that the preacher is forced to consider people, issues, and sociopolitical conditions that stretch over a period of one thousand years—issues that the preacher might otherwise have overlooked. There is no other genre of biblical literature that approaches the prophetic corpus in terms of the breadth of history and the depth of human experiences that are included among its pages. Sometimes Israel is at the height of its power and influence, and the message of the prophets is that God is about to bring that mighty nation to its knees because of its arrogance and pride. Other times the prophets issue a sweet call to Israel to return to the God whose love for them will not allow God to completely give up on them. The God who sent Hosea out to marry a prostitute named Gomer is the God whose love for us is stronger than our disregard for God.

ISSUES RAISED BY PROPHETIC PREACHING

The prophets remind Israel, just as we need to be reminded through regular doses of prophetic preaching, that God is the sovereign creator and sustainer of the whole creation. The God who sent Jonah to preach salvation in Nineveh is the same God who used first Babylon and then Persia as the instruments of God's will. The God who formed Israel into a great nation when its people were brought out of the brick pits of Egypt is the same God who can send Israel's people back into captivity. This is the same God who caused the people of Israel to hang their harps upon the willows and weep as they sat along the banks of the River Chebar and remembered the life they once lived in Zion. God's concern is for the whole of creation and for all the people that dwell therein. When the people of God lose sight of the goal and begin acting as if only they and their nation really matter, it is time for a prophet to declare, "Thus says God!"

In a nation whose religious life seemed overly focused on the Temple of Solomon, the Levitical priesthood, the careful observance of a legalistic lifestyle, and the proper practices of "holy living," prophetic preaching focused the people's attention on the issues that were broader than how to worship or where to pray or what it was lawful to eat. The Mosaic covenant included a series of clear commandments to care for the widows, the orphans, and the stranger among them. When the people of Israel lost sight of that commandment, the prophets were there to remind them.

Now as then, there is a need to lift up the conditions of widows, orphans, and strangers. Today they take the form of single women, many of them living in great poverty, who have been abandoned by husbands and boyfriends and are raising children by themselves. The world is literally awash with children who have been left orphaned by the unrelenting ravages of HIV/AIDS as well as by tribal warfare in Africa, ethnic cleansing in the Balkans, and wars in Iraq and Afghanistan that use the methods of terror (shock and awe) to combat acts of terrorism around the world.

The stranger is also among us today, though here too the forms have shifted. Now the strangers are the migrant workers who pick our food, the illegal immigrants who clean our homes and hotels, and the prisoners at Guantanamo Bay and inside of Abu Ghraib prison, who are under U.S. control but not afforded the protections of the U.S. Constitution. Further, these prisoners are without the protection of the Geneva Convention nor receive the common decency that any U.S. citizen would expect and/or demand. The stranger is also that person with an "Arab sounding name" or that Sikh from India who, because his religion requires him to wear a turban or some other kind of head wrap, is being caught up in the post–September 11, 2001, frenzy created and sustained by a government that is always on the lookout for a "person of interest."

THE DEMISE OF PROPHETIC PREACHING IN AMERICA

In the face of all that is currently happening in our world, it is shocking to note that the voice of the prophet is too rarely heard. True enough, biblical texts taken from the prophetic corpus are often employed in weekly sermons, but the power and the pathos are not heard or felt. Isaiah and Micah are used primarily to demonstrate that the birth of Jesus was foretold several hundred years earlier. Malachi is seldom preached except in an occasional sermon on tithing and the promise (3:10) that God will open the windows of heaven. We may hear from Zechariah (9:9) around Palm Sunday when the story is told of Jesus riding triumphantly into Jerusalem on a colt amid shouts of hosanna. The fiery words of the prophets, however, go unspoken in most pulpits across America. There is very little likelihood that the vast majority of those who hear sermons today will come out of their churches saying to one another, "The land is not able to bear all his words" (Amos 7:10).

In our postmodern society with its widespread biblical illiteracy, most people do not know and will likely never hear about Jeremiah's trip to the potter's house, his confinement in a cistern, or the yoke of oxen he wore around his neck to symbolize the bondage that was awaiting Judah if Jehoiakim and Zedekiah did not change their ways and the ways of the nation they ruled. They will probably not hear about the encounter between Nathan and David when the prophet told the king, "You are the man." They may never hear a sermon based upon Isaiah's condemnation of false gods and idolatry, or Ezekiel's warning from God that God's people were rebellious and impudent.

More than likely our people will hear sermons about the values of patriotism, the paths to peace and prosperity, the appropriate methods for baptism and communion, why God does not approve of women in ministry and why a woman's right to control her reproductive choices is the single greatest evil in the world today. Many of those who will preach such sermons are graduates of seminaries and schools of religion where you would think they would have been introduced to this body of biblical material. Many of them, however, will preach with no particular urgency or attention paid to the prophets because no such urgency was laid upon them when they sat in their classes in Bible, theology, ethics, or even homiletics!

PREACHERS—OFF IN OTHER DIRECTIONS?

A folk song of the 1960s raised this question in the context of the antiwar movement: where have all the flowers gone? There is a homiletical equivalent to that question that says:

> *Where have all the prophets gone?*
> *Gone in search of megachurches, every one.*
> *Where have all the prophets gone?*
> *Gone in search of faith-based funding, every one.*
> *Where have all the prophets gone?*
> *Gone in search of personal comfort, every one.*
> *Where have all the prophets gone?*
> *Gone in search of political correctness, every one.*
> *Where have all the prophets gone?*
> *Gone into a ministry that places praise over speaking*
> *truth to power, every one.*
> *When will they ever learn? When will they ever learn?*[2]

The point that is being made here is that prophetic preaching is absent from the scene because too many of those whose responsibility it is to raise the issues of justice and righteousness have become distracted and pre-occupied with other topics and other aspects of ministry. It is not that what they are doing is unimportant, though sometimes it can be trivial or self-serving. It is simply that too many preachers are ignoring the issues and the urgency of prophetic preaching as they invest all of their time and energy and imagination in some of what James and Christine Ward referred to as obscuring the wider dimensions of the gospel.[3]

This book is designed to help identify some of the things that may have become distractions in the life and work of those who occupy the pulpits of America. It is also designed to make the case for the importance of prophetic preaching for our churches and for our whole society, and its incorporation into the preaching schedule of every person who regularly stands before a congregation to preach the gospel of Jesus Christ.

A BIBLICAL HERMENEUTICS

In his book *Interpreting God's Word in Black Preaching*, Warren Stewart reflects on two hermeneutic principles fashioned by James A. Sanders in the 1970s. Sanders wrote about the "constitutive" and the "prophetic" readings of scripture. Stewart says:

> In biblical times the constitutive reading of the Torah story, which was based on a supportive interpretation of the Word, gave Israel an identity and a purpose. As the moral as well as the historical context of Israel changed, Israel became in need of a challenging message that would call it back to its original purpose as God's elect. Israel, in such a state, was not in need of a supportive reading of the tradition. The establishment context of Israel called for a prophetic interpretation of the Torah story.[4]

The message of the prophets calls us back to our original purpose as the people of God. It reminds us of how we should have been living all along. It points out what we have become as a people. It then challenges us to return to the ways of our God, the way in which we had long ago promised we would walk.

In his 1963 book *Letter from a Birmingham Jail*, Martin Luther King Jr. embodies for us what it looks like to preach from the prophetic texts and to be a prophet in our midst. He wondered how white Christians could build churches that were so beautiful to behold and then practice something as ugly as racial segregation within those same structures.[5] No doubt the church spires he noticed as he traveled throughout the American south in the 1950s and 1960s sat atop buildings that were well staffed and well funded. They had a solid constitutive foundation. Those churches, however, were not focused on what was the central social issue of that generation. In fact, the people in those churches were the primary reason why racism, segregation, and the rule of law known as Jim Crow could last as long as it did in America. What those church people needed to hear was a prophetic word.

TEXT SELECTION IS NOT THE KEY

It cannot be too strongly stated that prophetic preaching does not demand or even require the use of a text taken from one of the prophetic books of the Old Testament. Nor does it require any reference to one of the prophets of the classical period that stretched from the eighth to the fifth centuries B.C.E. Many sermons have been preached from a text taken from a prophetic book that was more "pathetic" than "prophetic." This is usually the result of a preacher who did not have his/her focus on that which constantly occupied the biblical prophets, namely that God's people were living in disobedience to the covenant that had been established between God and God's people.

Prophetic preaching occurs when the preacher seeks to bring the will of God to the attention of the people of God and then, as Elizabeth Achtemeier observes, to challenge them "to trust their [God] in all circumstances and to obey him with willing and grateful hearts."[6] Prophetic preaching happens when the preacher has the courage to speak truth to power not only inside the church building but also in the streets and boardrooms and jail cells of the secular order. We must be willing to do this if we are to be faithful to and worthy of following in the footsteps of Samuel who confronted Saul, Nathan who confronted David, Amos who condemned Jeroboam, Jeremiah who challenged both Jehoiakim and Zedekiah, and John the Baptist who did not grow mute or meek in the presence of Herod Antipas.

A "POINT OF VIEW"

This approach to prophetic preaching is consistent with what Walter Brueggemann in his book *The Prophetic Imagination,* calls "prophetic consciousness."[7] He writes that the work of the prophet is to be able to project before the people "an alternative future to the one the king wants to project as the only thinkable one."[8] For Brueggemann, the Old Testament prophets had to contend with what he calls "royal consciousness." This "royal consciousness" represents "the deeply entrenched forces—political, economic, social or religious—of Israel."[9] They are the status quo, and they only offer to people a vision of the future that allows them to remain in power and requires that the masses of people remain marginalized in society. The work of the prophet is to combat that single vision and show that God can and will bring about a future different from that envisioned by the ruling elite.

In drawing the tension between "prophetic consciousness" and "royal consciousness," Brueggemann is reminding us that in the eighth century B.C.E. world occupied by prophets like Amos and in the sixth century B.C.E. world occupied by prophets like Jeremiah, not all of the preachers were prophets. Indeed, we are also reminded that not all people who call themselves or who are referred to as prophets are standing in the tradition of those preachers who spoke an unrelenting message of justice and righteousness.

The presence of Amaziah, an ally and defender of King Jeroboam, and of Hananiah, who served a similar role with and for Zedekiah, serve as the clearest indicators that the great Old Testament prophets whose words and work are so instructive to us today did not have the preaching platform to themselves. There were other voices being heard at that same time, other voices that were also cloaked in the title of being prophetic. There was a difference, however, between Amos and Amaziah and between Jeremiah and Hananiah.

Amaziah stood against Amos and told him to return to Tekoa and never again to preach in Bethel, "for it is the king's sanctuary, and it is a temple of the kingdom" (Amos 7:13). To add insult to injury, in the preceding verse (7:12) Amaziah told Amos to go back and "earn his bread" by preaching in Judah—a clear reference that Amaziah assumed that all of the so-called prophets were on someone's payroll, as he was very likely on the payroll of his monarch. This comment led Amos to declare, "I am no prophet, nor a prophet's son . . . and God said to me, 'Go, prophesy to my people Israel'" (Amos 7:14–15).

Prophesy the word of God is precisely what Amos did. He decried the abuse of the poor in an economic system that favored and rewarded those who were already rich. He condemned a class of people, referred to as cows of Bashan, whose personal comforts prevented them from feeling or caring about the poverty and misery being experienced by many of their own people. Amos also made it clear that the comfort class was in large measure responsible for that inequity in society.

Hananiah sought to persuade both the king and the country of Judah that the words of judgment spoken by Jeremiah were not true. Hananiah saw it as his mission to reassure both king and country that God was not displeased, that the enemy at the gate (the army of Nebuchadnezzar) would not triumph over Judah, and that the future of Judah and its royal line was secure. Hananiah was the son of a prophet and he, too, spoke with the opening phrase "thus says God." He seemed to have at least as much credibility and authority as Jeremiah, and yet they preach two widely different messages; one was constitutive and the other one was prophetic. One was based upon the preservation of the status quo that is the essence of royal consciousness and the other was fueled by the alternative vision of the future that is the heart and soul of prophetic consciousness.

TOO MANY HAVE A ROYAL CONSCIOUSNESS

It cannot be doubted that many pulpits across America are filled by preachers who operate out of a royal consciousness. I once heard a televised sermon by a popular Presbyterian preacher from Fort Lauderdale, Florida, who ended his pastoral prayer with the words, "God Bless America." In the sermon that followed, I heard no reference from that preacher about the 2000 presidential election and the voting fraud that occurred in Florida that resulted in the first ever "selection" of a president of the United States. Nor was anything said about the armed members of the Florida State Patrol who, at that time, were going to the homes of elderly African Americans who had been actively involved in Get-Out-the-Vote efforts for the 2004 election. This was an obvious attempt to intimidate black voter registration and to suppress black voter turnout in that swing state.

This particular preacher consistently operates within a constitutive and royal consciousness hermeneutic. He and so many of his colleagues who crowd the airwaves of cable television religious broadcasting are reaching an enormous audience with the message that all is well in America. They have hijacked the title of being evangelical. No longer does that word suggest a deep commitment to the authority of scripture, a burning passion for spiritual transformation in the lives of those who hear the gospel, and a solid separation of church and state. Now, as a result of the stance of National Association of Evangelicals and preachers like the ones who are seen on television twenty-four hours a day, an evangelical is someone who holds a specific position on such issues as prayer in schools, abortion, school vouchers, capital punishment, affirmative action, and increased military

spending even if it is done at the expense of social programs. "God Bless America."

"EVANGELICAL" HAS BEEN HIJACKED

In twenty-first century America, a person who identifies
him- or herself as an evangelical is most likely to vote
Republican, vote against school levies for public school
districts, and stand opposed to funding the United
Nations because that agency encourages birth control in
parts of the world where poverty and overpopulation go
hand in hand. Many of today's evangelicals want a
smaller government in the United States but support the
overly aggressive Patriot Act that not only enlarges the
size and cost of the U.S. government but also greatly
threatens civil liberties and privacy.

Such persons are likely to have supported the war in
Iraq and the fall of Saddam Hussein, even though they also
likely know that twenty years earlier we equipped and encouraged that same Saddam Hussein when he was our ally
in a war that Iraq was fighting against Iran. The same could
be said about some persons who likely supported the war in
Afghanistan against the Taliban, Al Qaeda, and Osama bin
Ladin, despite the fact that we encouraged and equipped
them in their war against the Soviet Union during that
same point in history. U. S. foreign policy twenty to thirty
years ago laid the foundation for most of the turmoil in
which our nation is engaged today. That being said, those
"evangelical" preachers in America who have the largest
following and the highest name recognition seem to have
nothing to say on matters of justice and righteousness.
Where have all the prophets gone?

AN ALTERNATIVE VISION

What is needed in America is an alternative voice that
sets forth God's alternative vision for the future. While
$400 billion have been allocated to rebuild Iraq—after we

needlessly blew the country up with our shock and awe—there are forty-five million Americans that have no health insurance. While nearly $1 billion was spent on the 2004 election by candidates pursuing elective office at the federal level alone, a ban on assault weapons will be lifted without much congressional debate, and the minimum wage laws leave many working Americans in the status of the working poor. And today, newly established overtime laws in the workplace will allow employers to require overtime from their workers without paying them an overtime wage.

The abuse of the poor by the rich, the neglect of the neediest in our society, and the focus of a religious life that is defined by the proper performance of rituals and not the dogged pursuit of righteousness is where we find ourselves in America in the early years of the twenty-first century. It was times similar to these that spawned the biblical prophets and also the prophets who flashed across the stage of history: Sojourner Truth, Martin Luther King Jr., Desmond Tutu, Oscar Romero, Fannie Lou Hamer, William Sloane Coffin, and Philip and Daniel Berrigan. There are a lot of people preaching in this country and throughout the world today, but one feels the need to raise the question "where have all the prophets gone?"

THE AFRICAN AMERICAN CHURCH—EQUALLY SILENT

Lest this study be accused of focusing all of its attention outside of the black community, rendering black people more as victims than as perpetrators of the constitutive hermeneutic, let me say a word or two about what is happening in the pulpits of black churches across the country. It can best be described by the phrase, "All the prophets have turned to praising." I recently heard an announcement about a cruise that was being planned to the Caribbean that is to include presentations by many of the biggest names in the black community in the fields of entertainment, business, motivational speaking, and sports. The advertisement then said, "Get your praise on with the biggest names in the black church today." They then listed such names as Noel Jones, Creflo Dollar, Eddie Long, and others. I am not condemning any of those persons or the ministries in which they are engaged. I am expressing concern that the focus within so many black churches has shifted away from justice and righteousness to "getting your praise on." That is precisely what Amos was condemning when he uttered these words from God:

> *Take away from me the noise of your songs,*
> *I will not listen to the melody of your harps,*
> *But let justice roll down like waters,*
> *And righteousness like an everflowing stream.*
> (Amos 5:23–24)

What has happened to the legacy of Vernon Johns, Martin Luther King Jr., Howard Thurman, Samuel Proctor, Adam Clayton Powell Jr., and James Lawson? Where are the successors to Richard Allen, Nannie Helen Borroughs, Fannie Lou Hamer, and Prathia Hall? Why is it that more black preachers today are interested in helping people "get their praise on" than they are in getting schools improved, or getting the levels of poverty in the community right around their church reduced, or getting the rate of divorce lowered, or getting more and more black men into school and out of prison? One has to labor long and hard these days to hear a prophetic word even from within the African American church—that part of the body of Christ that forty short years ago had the audacity to see as its mission the goal of "saving the soul of America."

PRAISE SONGS CANNOT FIX WHAT'S WRONG

The black community in America is in what may be its greatest crisis since slavery. That community faces record levels of poverty, drug addiction, and alcohol abuse, and a staggering and constantly escalating rate of imprisonment usually for drug-related offenses. So many of the finest young men and women in our community make a foolish mistake related to the use or possession of the smallest imaginable amounts of illegal substances. They are convicted of a felony offense, and even if they receive a shortened sentence or drug abuse counseling in lieu of a prison term, they live the rest of their lives as ex-offenders. Such a phrase has the power to limit their hopes and dreams and their employment and upward mobility for as long as they live. It creates record levels of unemployment among adults and a staggering rate of teens that are both parents and high school dropouts.

These are the very real and urgent problems that confront millions of African Americans. There is certainly a need for praise and celebration as one way to cope with the problems that confront our community. The inspiration that come from times of praise and worship can go a long way toward helping people bear up under the weight and burden of these conditions. We cannot, however, let "getting our praise on become the sole or central reason for our coming together. We must speak to the issues that are the root causes of the social problems that we face. That is where prophetic preaching comes into play.

J. Deotis Roberts, writing in *Roots of a Black Future: Family and Church,* notes that the black church has traditionally operated out of two forms of ministry that he calls the priestly and the prophetic.[10] He says, "The priestly ministry of black churches refers to their healing, comforting, and succoring work. The prophetic ministry involves its social justice and social transforming aspects."[11] By being careful to include prophetic preaching in the course of a year's pulpit work, while continuing to allow people time to "get their praise on" black preachers can be sure that this historic and important balance in the worship and witnessing life of the black church continues into the future.

In speaking to those issues, black preachers must declare, "Thus says God" not only regarding what is being done to black people by white society. We must also say, "Thus says God" to our own community and our own congregations about the choices we are making and the values we are adopting that greatly contribute to our current dilemma. It must be remembered that as long as Amos was listing "for the three transgressions and four" against Moab, Edom, Syria, Gaza, and Judah, he was on safe ground in Bethel. It was when he turned his attention to the people who were present before him that his courage had to increase and his popularity suddenly fell.

PROPHETIC PREACHING TO YOUR OWN PEOPLE

It is not possible for a prophetic ministry to be sustained or for prophetic preaching to have authority when the words "This is what God says" are directed only toward those outside of the community in which the preachers live and work. While attention must be focused on the people and problems from the outside that are having a negative impact, attention must also be focused on the problems and the people within that community who are also doing harm as a result of their conduct and character. In other words, preachers must be willing not only to speak to leaders and policies at the national level, but to be equally forceful in addressing people and problems that reside within their local community and inside their local congregation.

Moreover, prophetic preaching cannot be limited to evils and injustices perpetrated by persons outside of the racial or ethnic group of the preacher. Equal attention must be given to the obvious, but often overlooked, evils and injustices that occur within the preacher's own racial and/or ethnic community. This is of special urgency for

African American preachers who have been leveling prophetic pronouncements against the things they see and object to in the broader American society. Many preachers within this community are long overdue in speaking out against black-on-black crime, the steadily increasing rate of teen pregnancy, the vile language of so much of the music that shapes the values of our children, and the frequent instances of black male underachievement in school because academic success is widely viewed in urban schools as "acting white."

PROPHETIC PREACHING WITH HOPE AND HUMILITY

Prophetic preaching requires something more than righteous indignation over what is happening in society and over what is not happening within the church. As Abraham Joshua Heschel wrote in his classic book *The Prophets*, "prophetic preaching must be endowed with 'divine pathos.'"[12] Heschel states, "The prophets communicated God's anger over the sins of the covenant community. However, what God intends is not that his anger should be executed, but that it should be annulled by the people's repentance."[13] In the final analysis, it is hope and deliverance, not death and destruction, that are the ultimate objectives of prophetic preaching. As Israel learned in 722 B.C.E. and as Judah learned in 586 B.C.E., death and destruction came not because God willed it, but because the people of God refused to listen to what the prophets were saying.

Prophetic preaching also requires a large amount of humility and the awareness that the sins we see in the people who hear the sermons are also alive and at work in the people who preach the sermons. Preachers have no right to preach a prophetic word with their fist balled up and their index finger pointed out and away from themselves. We do not have the right to preach to people about their sins as if we who preach are somehow above and removed from the problem. The preferred approach is to preach about the sins and shortcomings that grip and pull all of us away from the love and loyalty we should be displaying toward God. Isaiah speaks for all of us when he says, "Woe is me! I am lost, for I am a [person] of unclean lips and I live among a people of unclean lips" (Isa. 6:5). My slave ancestors put it equally well when they encouraged every one, preachers included, to sing:

> *It ain't my mother,*
> *It ain't my father,*
> *But it's me, O Lord,*
> *Standing in the need of prayer.*

TWO

WHAT ARE THE ISSUES OF JUSTICE AND RIGHTEOUSNESS?

He has told you, O mortal, what is good;
and what does God require of you but to do justice,
and to love kindness, and to walk humbly
with your God?

—Micah 6:8

On April 24, 2005, a service called Justice Sunday was beamed by satellite from a church in Louisville, Kentucky, to other locations across the country. The event was sponsored by two groups closely linked to what the news media refers to as "conservative, evangelical Christians": Focus on the Family and the Family Research Council. The expressed point of this event was to rally their base of conservative Christians to oppose a filibuster then being threatened by Democratic members of the United States Senate who opposed some of President Bush's appellate court nominees.

James Dobson, the founder and president of Focus on the Family, said that "opposition to Bush judicial nominees was opposition to people of faith."[1] Senate Majority Leader Bill Frist of Tennessee spoke to the group via satellite. He created a fascinating and dangerous partnership of certain elements of church and state around what in the end constitutes a narrowly defined social agenda. At the center of that political rally were the issues of abortion and human sexuality.

On August 14, 2005, a second rally, called Justice Sunday II, was held in Nashville, Tennessee. This event was sponsored by the same two groups and featured House Majority Leader Tom DeLay of Texas. The focus of the second rally was to "call attention to the Supreme Court's hostility to Christianity and traditional families in its decisions about abortion, homosexuality, and government support for religion."[2]

Something significant, however, had happened between those two events. By the second, Justice Sandra Day O'Connor had retired from the Supreme Court.

Conservative, evangelical Christians were anxious to see President Bush nominate someone who would, on the one hand, oppose any changes to the traditional definition of marriage—one man and one woman. On the other hand, the religious right also wanted federal judicial appointees who would rule to reduce a woman's access to reproductive choice. The special urgency concerning the replacement for O'Connor presented an opportunity to create a pro-life majority on the U.S. Supreme Court that would overturn the 1973 decision of Roe vs. Wade.

Two Justice Sunday events were held within the space of four months, and the common themes linking them together were the need for a federal judiciary that would uphold "moral values" so far as human reproduction and human sexuality are concerned. Opposition arose quickly to several possible replacements, including Attorney

General Alberto Gonzalez, "whose position on abortion they regarded as suspect."[3] John Robert Jr.'s nomination was shifted to fill the vacancy caused by the death of Chief Justice William Rehnquist. This left O'Connor's seat vacant for a nomination. Not surprisingly, both Harriet Myers and then Samuel Alito were immediately scrutinized concerning their views on these two issues.

WHAT ARE "MORAL VALUES"?

Those two Justice Sunday events called national attention to what the participants hailed as "moral values." A national dialogue about what constitutes "moral values" is important. The 2004 presidential election was largely framed by a debate about which candidate stood for and would work for "moral values." That phrase was heard as often as, if not more often than, the names of the candidates who were running for office. Many people would later state that the reason they voted for a particular candidate was because they liked that candidate's stand on "moral values." The question is, "What are these 'moral values'?" Of course, when examined more closely the issues that constitute "moral values" are the same as the ones that were at the heart of Justice Sundays: abortion and human sexuality.

JUSTICE: ONLY ABOUT ABORTION AND HUMAN SEXUALITY?

What is interesting to note is that there was not another, single issue that might come before the U.S. Supreme Court that was of interest to the conveners of Justice Sunday I or Justice Sunday II beyond abortion and same-sex marriage. Nothing was discussed about terrorism, the Patriot Act, immigration policy, environmental threats, or the residual concerns about voting irregularities carried over from the 2000 presidential election—an election where the U.S. Supreme Court virtually selected the president of the United States by canceling all vote recounting issues in Florida. Does the definition of justice in the twenty-first century begin and end with those two issues?

Nothing was said at either of the Justice Sunday events about the scourge of illegal drugs or the crime that is always associated with drug use. Nothing was said about the furor across the country attached to various proposals to determine whether or not the United States should designate English as its official language or require that everything from signs in public spaces to instruction in public schools should be offered also in Spanish. Nothing was said about federal sentencing guidelines that require judges to impose mandatory sentences without allowing for judicial discretion on a case-by-case basis.

The participants at both Justice Sunday events were equally silent on a host of other issues as well. There was no discussion on Justice Sunday about the quagmire that is the war in Iraq. Neither of those events discussed the lingering problems of racism or sexism in America. They did not comment upon the impact of urban sprawl on America's inner cities or upon land use policies that now have farmlands and super highways situated side by side. The definition of justice seems to have been limited to what those in attendance at Justice Sunday I and II called "moral values," and what others refer to as "a culture war."

What is most ironic is that Bill Frist, who was so visible in Justice Sunday I, was subsequently investigated for "insider trading" of shares he owned in a publicly traded company. Tom DeLay, who was visible and vocal at Justice Sunday II, was indicted in Texas for multiple violations of various campaign finance laws. He has since stepped down from his position as House Majority Leader and is not seeking reelection. No one from the leadership of either of those Justice Sunday events has spoken out about the behavior of either of these two men. Perhaps that is because they do not count charges of illegal stock market dealings or illegal campaign finance practices as being "justice" issues since neither case involves abortion or human sexuality.

These two issues are certainly of crucial importance in our society, no matter on which side of those issues a person may be. Opponents of abortion and especially of what is called late-term abortion feel a deep sense of outrage over what they see as the intentional killing of human life. Bioethicists and theologians must continue the important debate about when life begins: at conception or at birth. The issue is of immense importance to millions of Americans who hold to their views about the evil of abortion based upon their reading of scripture, and based just as much on what they see as a careless use of abortion as little more than another form of birth control.

On the other hand, there are people who object to the notion that abortion and being pro-choice are synonymous terms. People who are pro-choice are primarily interested in reducing the role of the government when it comes to making or limiting choices that they believe should be left to women in consultation with their physicians, families, and clergy. It is hard for pro-choice people to hear so much talk about the need for a smaller and less intrusive federal government, and then watch while that government seeks to intrude into what seems, to many Americans, to be a personal matter of the utmost privacy.

It is clear why any change in the U.S. Supreme Court could thrust this issue into the center of our national discussion. This is the reason why the matter was so central to the Justice Sunday events. The federal courts in general, and the U.S. Supreme Court in particular, were at the center of their concern. Of course, it is interesting that many of the same people who oppose an activist, federal judiciary (that makes the law instead of interpreting the Constitution) are trying to achieve precisely that kind of court with the appointment of the next Supreme Court justice.

James Dobson says, "There is a majority on the U.S. Supreme Court that is unaccountable and arrogant and imperious and determined to redesign the culture according to its own biases and values."[4] Of course, that is precisely what Dobson and Tony Perkins of the Family Research Council are trying to do at their Justice Sunday events. They purposely choose to place an emphasis on "moral values"—"moral values" that never seem to extend beyond the issues of abortion and various aspects of human sexuality.

The U.S. Constitution does not explicitly speak about either of these issues. This means that there is no article or amendment the court can "interpret according to the intent of the founders" or according to the "strict constructionist" philosophy. When conservative, evangelical Christians seek to create a federal judiciary after their own ideological image, they are looking for activist judges who will "legislate from the bench" in ways that meet their approval. How else can they hope to ban legalized abortion: a choice with which the vast majority of Americans are in agreement?

Alongside the debate raging over abortion between pro-life and pro-choice advocates is the even more intense debate about human sexuality in general and same-sex marriage in particular. Many who speak about this issue from both sides of the question actually feel themselves to be engaged in prophetic preaching. For some, the issue is the biblical definition of marriage as traced to Genesis 2:24–25 as "one man and one woman." This group would likely point to the words of Genesis 1:28 and the challenge to the first human couple to "be fruitful and multiply and fill the earth." That is a practice that opponents of same-sex marriage would point to as posing an obvious problem. How can persons of the same sex obey that commandment?

For others, the issue is as clear and as compelling as the language of the Fourteenth Amendment to the U.S.

Constitution and the claim of "equal protection under the law." Rights that are extended to some in this country should be extended to all. If marriage between a man and a woman brings with it certain rights, for example, hospital visitation, sharing in job-provided medical benefits, joint filing of tax returns, and many more, those who advocate for same-sex or same-gender marriage are seeking the same legal protections and rights for themselves.

It does not help the case of those who staunchly oppose same-sex marriage that the divorce rate for people in heterosexual marriage stands at about 50 percent. Even within the faith community, the rate of divorce is high. As Tony Campolo points out in his book *Speaking My Mind*, "Gays often ask why evangelicals seem willing to accept couples who are divorced and remarried, a sexual relationship that Jesus specifically condemned as adultery, then come down so hard on a sexual relationship that Jesus never mentioned."[5] This says nothing about the opposite-sex scandals that erupt in the public eye every day. In a world marred by cable TV stations, hotel movie channels, and dozens of magazines that cater to the sexual fantasies of heterosexuals at a cost that surpasses the amount that Americans spend on all professional sports combined, is homosexuality really the only sexual behavior that conservative, evangelical Christians see as a concern? I wonder if anyone who attended Justice Sunday or Justice Sunday II also watches *Desperate Housewives*?

SHALL WE ENFORCE LEVITICUS?

Most of the condemnation of homosexual conduct is tied to the language of Leviticus 18:22. If the church is being called upon to condemn homosexuality on the basis of the Holiness Code found in Leviticus 17–26, should we not be prepared to enforce all of the prohibitions and commandments found there? That would include the ones about not eating food with blood still present, as

with a rare steak (17:10–14); a man not having intimate relations with his wife during her menstrual cycle (18:19);
leaving portions of every agricultural field unharvested so
the poor can come and be fed (19:9–10); punishing the act
of adultery with the death of both parties (20:10); as well
as observing the Sabbath laws, Passover, and Pentecost as
an agricultural festival.

If the laws regarding same-sex conduct are viewed as
inviolate, then what about the laws governing the sabbat-
ical year when fields should not be sown or harvested or
the Jubilee Year when debts should be forgiven and prisoners should be released (25:1–7 and 8–17)? If the Bible is
our guide on homosexual conduct, then it should also
guide us in our treatment of the *sojourners* or *strangers* or
migrant workers or *illegal immigrants* among us whom we
work so hard and treat so unfairly (19:33). Of course,
under this reading of scripture everyone who condemns
homosexuality based upon the Levitical Code would likewise have to abstain from eating rabbit, pork, shrimp,
lobster, and other shellfish (11:6–11). What does this
mean for hunters who hate homosexuals but who shoot
and then handle the carcasses of animals that the
Levitical Code calls unclean (11:24–40)?

How is it possible that the only part of Leviticus that
modern-day evangelicals want to enforce with vigor and
venom is the portion dealing with homosexuality? What
do they presume to do with all of the other teachings?
This problem becomes even more critical for those who
cling to the "inerrancy" and "infallibility" of all scripture
on the one hand, but then pick and choose which portions and passages they will target for enforcement.

SHALL WE ENFORCE ROMANS 1?

The other biblical text regularly invoked to condemn homosexuality and homosexuals is Romans 1:26–27. That
text does not stand alone; it must be read as part of a

larger pericope that the critics of homosexuality often overlook or ignore. Nothing was said at Justice Sunday about *envy, greed, malice, gossip, slander, arrogance, insolence,* or *disobedience to parents.* If homosexuality is the great sin that so many conservative, evangelical Christians consider it to be, then who among them, according to Leviticus 17–26 or Romans 1:26–31 can cast the first stone?

It is this selective reading of scripture that is the real abomination in our society! This willingness to focus on and/or condemn as abomination some behaviors mentioned in scripture while ignoring, overlooking, tolerating, or freely engaging in other behaviors that are mentioned only a few verses later in the same chapter lies at the heart of the problem. People guilty of racism, sexism, national chauvinism, as well as "selective enforcement" of Levitical laws are as sinful as the people whose behaviors they presume to condemn.

HOMOPHOBIA: THE LAST ACCEPTED PREJUDICE?

What is of concern here is not limited to the issue of homosexual conduct or same-sex marriage. What is of equal concern is the gay-bashing and the open hostility toward gay and lesbian people that seems to have surfaced in America in the wake of the same-sex marriage discussion. What should the attitude of the church be toward gay and lesbian people? What should the church's position be toward openly gay and lesbian people serving in the various levels of ministry from pastors to bishops? Is the issue of homosexuality or the emotion known as homophobia "the last acceptable prejudice in America" as was suggested by the columnist Cynthia Tucker in October of 2004?[6]

This issue is too central to the life of our churches and our society to be ignored or swept under the rug. We certainly need some prophetic preaching to help us find our way, or better yet to help us find God's way in the face of these two issues. While we are doing this, both sides in the debate could do with a little humility when it comes to their quick assumption that their view and their view alone is God's position on the issue.

PETER GOMES AND HOMOSEXUALITY

I know of no preacher in America today who has been more forthright in an attempt to give shape and context to the issue of homosexuality and the Christian faith than Peter Gomes, minister at the Memorial Church at Harvard University. In an essay in *The African American Pulpit* and in a chapter in his 1996 release entitled *The Good Book*, Gomes not only speaks openly about his own homosexuality, but he also offers several angles and perspectives from which those biblical texts presumed to deal with the issue of homosexuality can be reconsidered.[7] Central to the position of Peter Gomes is the belief that, contrary to popular opinion, the Bible does not have an antigay bias. He writes:

> I happen to believe that our attitudes toward homosexuals and homosexuality are not based upon the Bible, although they appear to be because of the way in which we read the Bible. Those views come from the culture. Cultures, however, come and go: they are not absolute nor are they infallible. What is culturally true in one era—chattel slavery, for example—is manifestly untrue in another.[8]

Gomes calls for an end to what he calls "biblical homophobia," and asserts that getting American society to consider the issue of homosexuality from the point of view he is setting forth will be "one of our theological challenges in the twenty-first century."[9]

JUSTICE CANNOT BE LIMITED TO TWO ISSUES

Having acknowledged the importance of the debate that is going on within the church and throughout society on the issues of abortion and human sexuality, this book still wants to make one observation so far as prophetic preaching is concerned that the justice agenda in America is not and should not be limited to these two topics. The concern being raised by this book is not with the issues that some self-described "conservative Christians" have chosen to embrace and that those who call themselves "liberal" or "progressive" Christians have likewise identified as important, even though they view those issues differently.

In both instances, it is their right to pursue those issues even if both sides think the other side is wrong. The concern being raised here is with the impact on preaching in America as a result of a narrow and limited understanding of the word justice that seems to be in evidence not only at both Justice Sunday events, but also throughout the body of Christ in particular and American society in general. The absence of a prophetic voice in the pulpits of America may be related to this steadily narrowing definition of justice concerns to two issues, which leaves a wide area of concerns unaddressed and unresolved.

The question that remains is, what are the Justice Sunday advocates prepared to call justice issues beyond these two topics? Let us assume for the sake of argument that those who oppose reproductive choice, homosexuality, or same-sex marriage had their way and everything they abhorred about those issues was resolved to their full and complete satisfaction. Would that result in a perfect society? Would the removal of those two things usher in the reign of God on the earth? Or would the work of justice still need to go on and would the voice of the prophet still need to be heard?

A NARROW VIEW DIVIDES THE CHURCH

In whatever ways the focus on abortion and human sexuality may unite some who call themselves conservative, evangelical Christians, that narrow view of justice issues stands as a major obstacle to unity within the wider body of believers. It is the primary reason why all of the historically black Baptist and Methodist denominations have been reluctant to join a new ecumenical movement called Christian Churches Together in the USA (CCT). This new group is intended to bring together five branches of the Christian family tree: Roman Catholic, Orthodox, mainline Protestant, racial/ethnic, and evangelical/Pentecostal.

The Southern Baptist Convention has already announced that it has no intention of joining this group— perhaps because they fear it might push them beyond their "moral values" agenda. No black denomination has agreed to join either. Thomas Hoyt, the Christian Methodist Episcopal bishop of Louisiana and Mississippi and the president of the National Council of Churches, spoke to one reason why this is the case. He was concerned that some member churches would push "before birth" issues like abortion and others would push "after death" issues of eternal salvation. At the same time, the social and economic questions of life between the two would be brushed aside.[10] Hoyt said, "Those are critical issues of survival for us, that in-between time of jobs and food and clothing, and some people don't want to deal with those issues."[11]

IS THAT ALL THERE IS?

It must be restated that this is not an attempt to minimize the issues that are important to whomever falls under this definition of conservative, evangelical Christianity. Nor is this an attempt to condemn those who advocate for or against those issues. The question that I am raising is whether or not the definition of justice in the twenty-first century in the United States and around the world rises and falls on the issues of abortion and human sexuality. To quote from the song "Send in the Clowns," "Is that all there is?"

The answer to that question must be a resounding "NO!" Prophetic preaching must embrace many more issues than these two concerns. Too many who occupy the pulpits of America are preaching a woefully truncated gospel. Even if this network of conservative, evangelical Christians achieved the vision of America they are currently pursuing, the very next day the country would still need a prophetic voice to stand up and declare "Let justice roll down like waters and righteousness like an everflowing stream" (Amos 5:24).

A NARROW VIEW OF JUSTICE ON DISPLAY

This narrow definition of justice was clearly revealed in two side-by-side columns on November 24, 2005, in the *Atlanta Journal and Constitution*. One column dealt with the decision by the Georgia affiliate of the Southern Baptist Convention to sever its ties with and withdraw $3.5 million in scholarship funds from Mercer University. This action was taken because that historic Southern Baptist school had once allowed a gay student club on its campus. Further, this action was taken even though the gay students had already disbanded their club because they did not want their organization to put the university at odds with the Georgia Baptist Convention.[12]

In the parallel column there was a discussion about the continuing voting rights problems in Georgia, where members of the Georgia legislature were trying to require that photo identification be shown by anyone attempting to vote at their assigned polling station. Since 1965, Georgia has been under the scrutiny of the U.S. Department of Justice for denying African Americans the right to vote or obstructing that right. An attorney for the Department of Justice has recommended that this pending legislation not be approved for precisely that reason.[13] Nothing was said in either column about the support by Southern Baptists in Georgia to uphold the voting rights of all people in that state. Nothing was said about the Georgia Baptist Convention taking a stand against anything that even hints at a violation of the 1965 Voting Rights Act. Here again, there is a major Christian body identified with the conservative, evangelical movement that operates within a narrow definition of justice. A school can be punished by a church group for having once allowed a gay student organization on campus, but that same church group voices no opposition to voting rights violations.

The message is even more drastic because many Baptist-related schools and seminaries have been similarly punished for holding views or tolerating opinions different from the creedal statement of the Southern Baptist Convention. The next generation of Baptist clergy and lay leaders are being shaped and molded within this definition of justice. They are being shown that any attempt to think outside the boundaries of present Southern Baptist thinking will result in a severe reprisal. These are the same Southern Baptist churches that caused Martin Luther King Jr. to wonder "what kind of Christians" worship in churches that are so beautiful on the outside and so segregated on the inside.[14] Is the punishment of a historic Baptist university that once allowed a now defunct gay student association really the issue with which twenty-first-century Christians should be concerned?

MAINLINE DENOMINATIONS JUST AS GUILTY

What should be of great concern to the church and to the nation as a whole is that this preoccupation with two issues of the culture wars is no longer limited to certain conservative, evangelical Christians. The same can increasingly be said about the mainstream Protestant denominations that gave birth to the likes of Clarence Jordan and William Sloane Coffin, John Bennett and Reinhold Niebuhr, Martin Luther King Jr. and Joan

Brown Campbell. You do not hear as much prophetic preaching coming from this branch of the body of Christ where lions once roared and where a wide definition of justice was demanded and pursued.

The mainline Protestant church was home to Henry Ward Beecher, who gave expression to his antislavery views by holding mock slave auctions at his church in Brooklyn Heights, New York, in the 1840s and 1850s. The mainline Protestant church is where Harry Emerson Fosdick took his stand against war following the horrors of World War I. Even here, one must ask the question, "Where have all the prophets gone?" The answer is that many of them have become drawn into the very same narrow definition of justice.

Bill McKibben, writing in the August 2005 issue of *Harper's Magazine,* observes: "The mainline Protestant churches that supported civil rights and opposed the war in Vietnam are mostly locked in a dreary decline as their congregations dwindle and their elders argue endlessly about gay marriage and same-sex unions."[15] To prove his point, one need only look at the news report covering the issues that have occupied those mainline groups over the last two years.

EPISCOPALIANS, UNITED METHODISTS

In 2003, the 2.3 million-member Episcopal Church in America was known for little else than its decision to consecrate an openly gay man, V. Gene Robinson, as the bishop of New Hampshire. In 2005, the leaders of the Episcopal Church issued a 130-page paper that justified their actions concerning Robinson as well as their decision to bless same-sex unions that they affirm as possessing "genuine holiness."[16] Following this act, in November 2005, a conservative movement within the Episcopal Church of about twenty-four hundred bishops, clergy, and lay members announced the intent to remove itself from that church body. They proposed a new structure that would come under the jurisdiction of other bishops within the worldwide Anglican Communion who conform to the "traditional views" of human sexuality.[17]

What is being addressed in this book is not the views of the Episcopal Church on the related issues of homosexuality, but rather what else is on the agenda of the Episcopal Church beyond this issue? What other statements of concerns or resolutions have they set forward on the other justice issues that confront this nation and the world? If they have addressed other concerns, they are not being heard within American society because of all the attention that is being devoted to this one area.

The Episcopal Church is by no means alone. Since 1972, every quadrennial meeting of the 8.3 million-member United Methodist Church has struggled with the issue of homosexuality. In 2000 in Cleveland and 2004 in Pittsburgh, it was front page news for each week-long conference. In a series of actions taken in 2005, the Council of Bishops of the United Methodist Church ruled that homosexuality is not a barrier to church membership. The same, however, cannot be said about their views concerning openly gay clergy. The United Methodist Church has voted to disallow the ordination of openly homosexual persons to the ministry.[18] The church's Judicial Council reinforced that position in October of 2005 when it voted to defrock an openly lesbian pastor.[19]

UCC, AMERICAN BAPTISTS, EVANGELICAL LUTHERANS

In July 2005, the 1.3 million-member United Church of Christ (UCC) endorsed same-sex marriage at its General Synod in Atlanta. At the same time, the 1.5 million-member American Baptist Churches, during their meeting in Denver, worked feverishly to avoid a split over the issue of homosexuality and the ordination of gay and lesbian clergy. A few weeks later, the 4.9 million-member

Evangelical Lutheran Church in America approved a resolution that allowed sexually active gay and lesbian clergy to remain in the pastoral ministry of that denomination.

THE REFORMED CHURCH IN AMERICA

The nearly three hundred thousand-member Reformed Church in America fired Norman Kansfield as president of its New Brunswick Theological Seminary in New Jersey, then defrocked him because he presided at the same-sex marriage of his daughter without first informing the school's Board of Trustees. At the same time, David Myers of RCA-affiliated Hope College in Michigan co-authored a book with Letha Dawson Scanzoni entitled *What God Has Joined Together? A Christian Case for Gay Marriage.* One RCA pastor said about the book, "It's going to pour some fuel on the fire. On the other hand, if we can have civil discussions on whatever points he makes, and debate in a good Christian way, then the church can be stronger for it."[20]

WHAT ELSE DO MAINLINE CHURCHES STAND FOR?

The same question directed earlier to conservative, evangelical Christians must also be directed to these mainline denominations: What else have the mainline churches been talking about and working on beyond this single issue of human sexuality? What have they been saying about economic justice, race relations, the outsourcing of American jobs, the state of the environment, the role of women in the church, or the war in Iraq and the related charges of torture of prisoners of war and "enemy combatants"? What are they doing about the scourge of HIV/AIDS, the staggering number of persons confined in America's prisons, the fact that forty-six million people in America have no medical insurance, or the explosion of divorce and teen pregnancy in America? The central claim in this chapter is that the major interests of

America's religious communities are reflected every day in the various news media of our nation. I am sure they have been speaking out on these wider issues of justice, but their voices are not being heard, their views are not being reflected, and their presence is not being felt. That is primarily because they and the national new media have become fixated on their actions and reactions concerning a narrow definition of justice.

Once again, this is not meant to minimize the importance of the issues they are addressing, but rather to reinforce that the definition of justice must be broader than the one or two topics shaping the debate about justice in mainline churches in the last three years. In previous generations, mainline Christians took aim not only at the issue of racism and the call for an integrated society, but they also spoke out against the war in Vietnam. Further, many mainline denominational leaders were actively involved in the advocacy group then known as Clergy and Laity Concerned about Vietnam. Martin Luther King Jr. not only led the American civil rights movement but he was also a leader in the antiwar effort from 1966 to 1968.

JACKSON, MISSISSIPPI, REVISITED

As a reminder of the kind of things that once concerned mainline Christianity, *Jet* magazine reported on a reunion of twenty-eight United Methodist ministers from Mississippi who had jointly issued a document in 1963 called "Born of Conviction." In that document, they denounced the racism that was so rampant in the South at that time. Some of them were dismissed by their congregations. Others were forced to flee Mississippi under death threats. A few of them remained in Mississippi and fought it out.

One of those ministers, Rev. Keith Tonkel, who has led the interracial Wells United Methodist Church in Jackson for thirty-six years, explained why he decided to remain in the eye of the storm. "How can you flesh out a conviction if you are absent? I thought our responsibility was to see what we can create that would be inclusive."[21] Out of the twenty-eight who signed the document in 1963, eight are dead and the rest are retired. Who will rise up and take their place, bringing a voice of courage and conviction to the equally pressing issues of our generation? Even within the once social justice–driven denominations of mainline Protestant Christianity the question must be raised: Where have all the prophets gone?

AFRICAN AMERICAN CHURCHES

As an African American pastor of more than thirty years, I must in all honesty confess that a narrow focus on "moral values" as a substitute for a broader and more comprehensive justice agenda is not a problem only for white conservative, evangelical Christians or for white, mainline Protestant denominations. With increasing frequency, many in the African American Christian community are adopting a similar view of justice issues. Their views echo the "moral values" argument of the 2004 election or that in the Justice Sunday rhetoric in the two 2005 gatherings in Louisville and Nashville.

FROM JUSTICE SUNDAY TO THE BLACK CONTRACT WITH AMERICA

Barbara Reynolds, the seminary trained columnist for *USA Today*, writes: "At a time when black America is in murky, troubled waters, too many of the black clergy, especially those heading mega churches, are either apolitical or apologists for the status quo."[22] She notes the formation of the newly established High Impact Leadership Coalition that has unveiled its Black Contract with America. Headed by Bishop Harry Jackson of Maryland, the group also includes such high-profile black church figures as Bishop Charles Blake of the twenty-five-thousand-member West Angeles Church of God in Christ and the Rev. Frederick Price of the Crenshaw Christian Center, both in Los Angeles, California. The stated goal of that group is to focus African Americans on moral issues.

Despite all of the issues plaguing black communities across the country, this group has named opposition to same-sex marriage as its top priority. In the face of an HIV/AIDS pandemic, staggering rates of unemployment, black-on-black crime, increasing teen pregnancy rates, and the rapid spread of Islam as the religion of choice among many young men within inner city neighborhoods, how is it possible that their top priority could possibly be same-sex marriage?

While campaigning in Miami, Florida, for John Kerry during the 2004 presidential campaign, Jesse Jackson raised this issue with a black church congregation of about five hundred people: "How many of you or someone from your family married somebody of the same sex?" When no one in that congregation raised his or her hand, Jackson then asked, "Then how did that (same-sex marriage) get in the middle of the agenda?"[23] That is a question begging for an answer, since instances of the degradation of black women in hip-hop music and videos are far more common and of much greater consequence than the almost negligible interest in same-sex marriage among African Americans.

What happened to voices like Nannie Helen Burroughs of the Women's Department of the National Baptist Convention? Not only was she pursuing an equal role for black women in that black Baptist convention in 1900, but she was also challenging white women in America to use their influence to bring an end to racism.[24] What happened to voices like Prathia Hall? She was a leader in the Student Non-Violent Coordinating Committee (SNCC) and a freedom rider in the 1960s. She was also an advocate for the role of women in the Progressive National Baptist Con-

vention in the 1970s and 1980s, and an early advocate for
Womanist Theology in the 1990s and into the twenty-first
century.[25] These were women with wide interests and a
broad and aggressive justice agenda.

WHEN WILL AMERICA PRACTICE WHAT IT PROFESSES?

Bill McKibben in that same *Harper's Magazine* article
mentioned previously offers another insight into the state
of religion in America. He says, "America is simultane-
ously the most professedly Christian of the developed nations and the least Christian in its behavior."[26] He notes
that over 85 percent of all Americans identify themselves
as Christians, and yet this country leads all developed nations in the murder rate, the use of capital punishment,
the number of persons incarcerated, the percentage of
marriages ending in divorce, the rate of teen pregnancy,
and the number of children living in poverty.[27] Perhaps if
we could move beyond our national fixation with abortion and human sexuality we could focus on these other
embarrassments in our national life. Prophetic preaching
would call for just such a response.

THERE ARE EXCEPTIONS ON BOTH SIDES

It must be stated and restated that there are many persons
who are conservative, evangelical Christians who do not
subscribe to the Justice Sunday agenda. There are many
good people who proudly wear the banner of mainline
Protestant who are not locked in to the two issues of
abortion and same-sex marriage. It can only be hoped
that their voices and concerns can be heard above the arguments that seem to be the focus of so many Christians
and for much of the media at present.

THREE

From "Moral Values" to Biblical Justice

*I was hungry and you fed me, I was thirsty
and you gave me something to drink, . . . I was naked
and you gave me clothing, I was sick and you took care
of me, I was in prison and you visited me.*

— Matthew 25:35–36

In order to broaden our discussion of "moral values,"
let us look to the passage known as the Great Judgment
scene in Matthew 25:31–44. In that passage, Jesus lists
several areas of human concern—hunger, thirst, lack of
sufficient clothing, sickness, prison—in which those who
are his disciples would surely be involved. Jesus also
identified himself with a group of people he called "the
least of these."

Thus, for Jesus, justice involves acts of compassion
and concern that are extended to those in the community
who are the neediest, the most vulnerable, and the most
at risk of having no advocate. These issues constitute the
"moral values" of Jesus. How ironic that nothing was said

by the advocates and promoters of Justice Sunday about these issues that Jesus explicitly identified as being of most importance to him.

It should be noted that failure to act upon the justice agenda of Jesus has a consequence, no matter what other issues we may choose to pursue instead. Those who refuse to involve themselves in these areas listed in Matthew 25:31–44 are likely to hear Jesus say to them, "You that are accursed, depart from me" (25:41). Jesus causes the issue of justice to swing on two hinges: one hinge is the action that people of faith should engage in on behalf of "the least of these," and the other is the accountability that awaits those who fail to act.

It is not optional and it is also not inconsequential whether or not we as Christians engage in the work of justice. There is God's blessing to receive when we do so and there is God's judgment to face when we do not. In any discussion of biblical justice it is important to make this point about action and accountability—about the help and support and relief we should offer to those in need and the judgment of God that awaits us when we fall short of that responsibility.

DISTRIBUTIVE AND RETRIBUTIVE JUSTICE

Charles Colson, formerly of Watergate fame during the Nixon administration and now the head of Prison Fellowship Ministry, offered a keen insight into the two-dimensional nature of biblical justice. Following Justice Sunday I, at which he was in attendance and in full support, he appeared on a TV program with someone who was critical of the narrow justice agenda of that event. He reflected back on the 1960s when justice was viewed as "distributive," meaning that the resources of the nation were distributed or made available to people who were in need of assistance. He defined that brand of justice as people "getting their due or giving benefits to the needy." He pointed to Lyndon Johnson's Great Society and the various social welfare programs that Johnson created as representative of that kind of public policy. He noted that despite all the money spent on various programs—from hunger to housing to health care—distributive justice in that form did not bring an end to America's social problems.

He then noted that the 1970s and 1980s under Nixon, Ford, and Reagan introduced a different kind of public policy that focused on "law and order" or retributive justice, as in retribution. The heart of this brand of justice was "to punish wrongdoers"—to hold people accountable for their conduct by stronger enforcement of the law and more severe punishment for those who break the law. As a result of twenty-plus years of this policy, more people were put in jail for longer periods of time, but, once again, God's shalom was not established on the earth. Colson concluded that neither the distributive nor the retributive forms of justice were successful. This was largely because each of them tended to operate in isolation from the other. "Biblical justice recognizes that both punishment and meeting social needs are essential to a just society."[1]

THE CONTENT OF BIBLICAL JUSTICE

What Jesus and the biblical prophets did was link these two elements together. Therefore, the law that had to be followed involved the acts of compassion that should be displayed. People of faith in the Old Testament community were challenged to care for the widow, the orphan, and the stranger in their midst (cf. Deut. 24:19, Isa. 1:17, Jer. 7:6, Ezek. 22:7, Hos. 14:3, Zech. 7:10 and Mal. 3:5). As Colson notes, "ancient Israelites were told to leave gleanings at the side of the field for the poor (as in the book of Ruth) and maintain honest scales as called for by Ezekiel 45:10, with the failure to do so being condemned by Amos 8:5."[2]

Jesus extends this concept into the New Testament with his use of the term "the least of these" and his explicit list of the actions that should be undertaken on their behalf. Distributive justice involves the acts of caring and compassion for the neediest in our society, which we undertake as a matter of obedience and discipleship. Retributive justice is what God directs toward those who fail to do what has been commanded. There is something that we are commanded to do as disciples of Jesus Christ, and there is a consequence we may face if we fail to do as Christ commands.

FOR THREE SINS AND FOR FOUR . . .

This linkage between distributive and retributive justice is nowhere better joined together than in the opening passages of Amos and the famous lines "For three transgressions of Damascus, and for four, I will not revoke the punishment"(1:3a). The first six oracles are directed against foreign nations. Israel would have been delighted to learn that God was planning to punish them for their wickedness. The seventh oracle was directed against Judah, Israel's much despised cousins to the south. Not many tears would be shed if God heaped wrath upon their former covenant partners. The eighth oracle, however, and the one Amos had actually come to Bethel to deliver, was both delivered in Israel and directed against Israel, and it linked distributive and retributive justice together.

> *Thus says God:*
> *For three transgressions of Israel, and for four,*
> *I will not revoke the punishment;*
> *Because they sell the righteous for silver,*
> *and the needy for a pair of sandals—*
> *they who trample the head of the poor into the dust*
>   *of the earth,*
> *and push the afflicted out of the way;*
> *father and son go in to the same girl,*
> *so that my holy name is profaned. . . .* (Amos 2:6–7)

The same link between distributive and retributive justice is found in Ezekiel 18:10–13.

> If he has a son who is violent, a shedder of blood, who does any of these things (though his father does none of them), who eats upon the mountains, defiles his neighbor's wife, oppresses the poor and needy, commits robbery, does not restore the pledge, lifts up his eyes to the idols, commits abomination, takes advance or accrued interest; shall he then live? He shall not. He has done all these abominable things; he shall surely die; his blood shall be upon himself.

RECAPTURE THE TENSION

The great need that faces preaching today and that is badly needed by the people who hear that preaching is the reclaiming of this tension between action and accountability, between distributive and retributive justice, between obeying God's command to do the work of justice and facing God's judgment and wrath when we fail or refuse to do so. The pulpit must echo with that dual message that has been inherited from Amos and Jesus and that has now been passed down to those who occupy the pulpits today. There is a lifestyle that we as Christians have been called upon to live. This lifestyle is not limited to observing the proper rituals, or engaging in the appropriate observances, or adhering to strict interpretations of doctrine, or toeing the line when it comes to certain matters of personal morality and ethical conduct. This lifestyle must include our care and concern directed to the "least of these" in our society.

Prophetic preaching must remind people of faith that we live in community with one another, and with that community comes mutual responsibility and accountability. The poet John Donne wrote, "No man is an island entire of himself. . . . Every man's death diminishes me because I am involved in mankind."[3] Martin Luther King Jr. said, "We are caught up in an inescapable network of mutuality tied in a single garment of destiny. . . . Injustice anywhere is a threat to justice everywhere. Whatever affects one directly affects all indirectly."[4] Prophetic preaching should serve to push and prod the people of faith to assume some interest in and some responsibility for the lives and well-being of others on a wide range of issues.

BEYOND DOCTRINAL DISPUTES

The people who hear our sermons must regularly be challenged about issues beyond stewardship and giving 10 percent of their income. They must be challenged to understand their faith as involving more than the manner of their baptism or the method by which they share in communion. They must see that their support of denominational programs, while important, does not exhaust what it means to be a follower of Jesus. They must be encouraged to look at the suffering and exploitation and economic injustice going on all around them, and then hear someone from the pulpit cry aloud and say, "This is what God says" about those conditions. This can only happen when preachers and churches are prepared to see that their justice agenda must extend beyond the issues of abortion and human sexuality.

Of course, those other matters must be attended to over the course of a year's preaching. Attention must be given to those matters that Cleophus LaRue in his book *The Heart of Black Preaching* calls "domains of experience." This would allow for preaching on matters of personal piety, care of the soul, and congregational life and the maintenance of the institutional church. This system of text and topic selection, however, still leaves ample time for what LaRue calls social justice and corporate concerns.[5] Later in this book, I will give some guidance about how issues of justice and mutual responsibility can become a regular part of one's preaching schedule. At this point, suffice it to say that social justice extends to issues far beyond the culture war topics of abortion and human sexuality, and so must the prophetic preaching heard in this country.

POVERTY IN THE WORLD'S RICHEST NATION

It should be a justice issue that millions of Americans live at or below the poverty line in America. As a result of poverty, millions of people, most of them children, have an inadequate diet that results in increased sickness. That sickness is complicated by an absence of medical insurance for forty-five million people in this country. The best cure for poverty is a quality education and a job that pays a living wage. Regrettably, public education in America is in crisis, and that is especially true in urban and inner city neighborhoods, as detailed so compellingly by Jonathan Kozol's book *Savage Inequalities.*[6]

The jobs that are being created are largely found in office parks and factories in outer ring suburbs that are not serviced by public transportation, thus they are out of the reach of those most in need of a job. For those people teetering on the brink of poverty who do somehow manage to get access to cars, the skyrocketing cost of gasoline makes it nearly impossible for them to purchase the fuel to get them to their jobs. Many of these people are numbered among the working poor who have to hold down two or more minimum wage jobs just to make ends meet; and those jobs typically come with no benefits such as sick days. Thus, they live the most anxious of lives because they know that if they get sick, not only do they not have any medical insurance to treat their illness, but they can also lose one or both of their jobs.

PUBLIC POLICY AND AN OWNERSHIP SOCIETY

Many of these working poor as well as those who are more secure are left to wonder why their employers compensate them so poorly when the top executives earn more than twenty times the amount paid to their employees. President Bush wants to privatize Social Security so more people can own their pension plans; this is part of his larger concept of America as "an ownership society." In fact, in the words of President Bush as heard on *Good Morning America*, "Owning stuff is good."

Such a concept would be a laudable goal were it not so hard to own something when your job is being outsourced to China or India. It is hard to own something when 85 percent of the nation's wealth is controlled by 18 percent of the people. It is hard to own something when the monthly price of gasoline to fill your car's tank is higher than the monthly car payment itself.

It seems as if President Bush thinks the U.S. Constitution says, "We, the people who own stuff . . ." This issue takes us all the way back to 1787 and the ratification of the Constitution. At the founding of our republic, only white males over the age of twenty-one who owned one hundred acres of land or more were voting citizens. Everybody else was de facto second-class. It took this nation more than 140 years, a civil war, and the passage of the Nineteenth Amendment guaranteeing suffrage to women before we outgrew the elitist notion that only those who "own stuff" matter in this country.[7]

What do we say about the people in America who can no longer own the home they once lived in because, as a result of layoffs, downsizing, and outsourcing, they have no job and can no longer afford the expenses of ownership? There are millions of people in this country who do have jobs with benefits, but each month brings with it another announcement of a major U.S. corporation that is declaring its retirement fund and pension plans bankrupt as a result of mismanagement. These are the kinds of people and the kinds of practices that should receive the attention of prophetic preaching.

CORPORATE FRAUD AND ECONOMIC INJUSTICE

While conservative, evangelical Christians have been meeting on their justice agenda, the news media has been full of reports about Enron, Global Crossing, WorldCom, Tyco, Adelphia, and other major U.S. corporations that have been looted by their chief executive officers, leaving their workers and retirees in financial ruin. The upper level executives give themselves "golden parachutes" while the average workers must face their retirement years without the medical insurance and pension checks they had been counting on during the period in their lives when they would most likely need that protection.

I have rarely heard Focus on the Family or the Family Research Center offer any opinion on these "family values" concerns. Yet these are the real world issues that have the widest and most negative impact upon America's families. Whether it is steel workers who must compete against cheaper steel made in China or Germany, or locally owned family businesses that must compete against WalMart and its inventory of products from countries that pay low wages and observe few if any environmental regulations in the production of their goods, working class families in America are finding it harder to make ends meet. Nothing else matters so long as CEOs and their stockholders receive bigger dividends and bonus checks than they did the year before. We need to hear some prophetic preaching on issues like these, but none of this came up on either of the two Justice Sundays.

THE WORLD'S LARGEST PRISON POPULATION

I have not heard the leaders of Justice Sunday say anything about the fact that two million people occupy America's jails and prisons, making incarceration and prison construction twin boom industries in this country. Regrettably, this is the case even though 80 percent of the people who are incarcerated at an approximate cost of twenty-five thousand dollars per year would be much better served in a drug court program that could address their major behavioral problem. This could be done at a cost of five thousand dollars per year. It costs twice and sometimes three times the amount to incarcerate someone than it does to educate that person at a state university. It is bad social policy and bad economic policy; and yet that topic did not come up at either Justice Sunday event.

As has already been pointed out, part of prophetic preaching does deal with the issue of "retributive justice" or of being held accountable for one's actions. It seems, however, that the United States practices selective enforcement concerning this aspect of justice. The nation's prisons are crowded with poor, undereducated minority persons. African Americans constitute about 13 percent of the national population, and yet they constitute over 70 percent of the prison population. Is this really because African Americans commit 70 percent of the crimes in America? Or is it because so many persons caught in this cycle of poverty cannot afford a private attorney and end up with a public defender they meet one hour before they appear in court, one who urges them to take a plea for a lesser sentence?

RESTORATIVE JUSTICE

Another key element of prophetic preaching that was as present in the oracles of the prophets of the eighth to sixth centuries B.C.E. as it was in the preaching of Jesus some seven centuries later is the issue of how people should be treated who have sinned and suffered the consequences for their sins. People should not be made to suffer forever for the sins of their past. They should be shown "restorative justice." This is what God promised Israel in Isaiah 40:1–5 upon announcing the end of that nation's exile into Babylon as penalty for the sins of injustice and idolatry:

Comfort, O comfort my people, says your God.
Speak tenderly to Jerusalem, and cry to her
that she has served her term, that her penalty is paid,
that she has received from God's hand
double for all her sins. (Isa. 40:1–2)

As a result of the nation's failure to practice distributive justice the people had to endure God's retributive justice in the form of the destruction of their temple, the end of their monarchy, their removal from the promised land, and seventy years of exile in Babylon.

Their punishment, however, would not last forever. God would restore them into their homeland and offer them a new future in covenant relationship with the Sovereign who had punished them but was now about to restore them. The great desert between Babylon and Jerusalem that once served to separate the Israelites from their home was about to become an open road back home by the intervention of God.

A voice cries out:
"In the wilderness prepare the way of God;
make straight in the desert a highway for our God.
Every valley shall be lifted up,
and every mountain and hill be made low;
the uneven ground shall become level,
and the rough places a plain.
Then the glory of God shall be revealed,
and all people shall see it together. . . ." (Isa. 40:3–5)

Isaiah extends the interconnection of distributive, retributive, and restorative justice in 58:10–12 when he says:

If you offer your food to the hungry
and satisfy the needs of the afflicted,
then your light shall rise in the darkness
and your gloom be like the noonday.
. . . Your ancient ruins shall be rebuilt;

you shall raise up the foundations of many generations;
you shall be called the repairer of the breach,
the restorers of streets to live in.

A similar promise of restorative justice is given in Jeremiah 29:10–14. This passage, which is so often and mistakenly used by those who advocate for a cheap prosperity, actually deals with what God promises the people after they have suffered for their lack of distributive justice. The nation has a future, but that future is only revealed after the people have endured God's retributive justice.

> This is what God says: "When seventy years are completed for Babylon, I will come to you and fulfill my gracious promise to bring you back to this place. For I know the plans I have for you, declares God, plans to prosper you and not to harm you, plans to give you hope and a future. Then you will call upon me and come and pray to me, and I will listen to you. You will seek me and find me when you seek me with all your heart. I will be found by you, declares God, and will bring you back from captivity. I will gather you from all the nations and places where I have banished you, declares God, and will bring you back to the place from which I carried you into exile." (Jer. 29:10–14 NIV)

The message of God's restorative justice, of God's willingness to offer a new future and a second chance to those who have failed in the area of distributive justice and endured the ordeal of retributive justice is central to prophetic preaching. After all the sins mentioned by Hosea, God's last word to Israel is:

> *How can I give you up, Ephraim? How can I hand*
> *over, O Israel? . . . My heart recoils within me;*
> *my compassion grows warm and tender.* (Hos. 11:8)

After all the judgments pronounced by Amos, God's final words are:

> *On that day I will raise up*
> *the booth of David that is fallen,*
> *and repair its breaches,*
> *and raise up its ruins,*
> *and rebuild it as in the days of old;*
> *in order that they may possess the remnant of Edom*
> *and all the nations who are called by my name,*
> *says God who does this.* (Amos 9:11–12)

God takes our sins very seriously and holds us account-able for them. We are obliged to obey God's teachings and to live by God's commandments.

Part of prophetic preaching involves setting those teachings and commandments before God's people and challenging them to live out those principles and prac-tices in their daily lives. Another part of prophetic preaching is warning God's people of the consequences that can and may follow if they fail to or refuse to obey God. A third part of prophetic preaching, however, in-volves God's promise of restorative justice. Nowhere is that promise more beautifully stated than in Psalm 30:4–5, which says:

> *Sing to God, you saints;*
> *praise God's holy name.*
> *For God's anger lasts only a moment,*
> *but God's favor lasts a lifetime;*
> *weeping may remain for a night,*
> *but rejoicing comes in the morning.* (NIV)

Those who preach the Gospel of Jesus Christ would be hard pressed to avoid the issue of restorative justice, because Jesus himself extends that form of justice over and over again. The classic case would involve the woman caught in adultery in John 8:7–11. Jesus does not dismiss or minimize the sin with which the woman was being charged; but he does issue a challenge to those in that stone-carrying crowd; "Let anyone among you who is without sin be the first to throw a stone at her." Jesus was the only person in that crowd who could have legitimately cast a stone that day, but instead he stooped down in order to lift that woman up. "Go your way, and from now on do not sin again." With that phrase Jesus acknowledges the sin in the woman's life but then urges her to live differently in the future. Rather than having her be killed or forever condemned, Jesus restores her to the fellowship of the community. She has a future despite the sins of her past.

The same can be said about the story of Zaccheus the tax collector in Luke 19:1–10. After a lifetime of economic exploitation of his own people and of collaboration with the hated Romans, whose occupation of Palestine was made possible in part by the taxes Zaccheus was collecting and passing on to them, Zaccheus had an encounter with Jesus. The first thing that happened was that Zaccheus practiced retributive justice by repaying fourfold everything he had unfairly gained as a tax collector. After that acknowledgment of his sin and his own act of restoration, Jesus then extends restorative justice to Zaccheus: "Today salvation has come to this house, because he too is a son of Abraham. For the Son of Man came to seek out and to save the lost" (Luke 19:9–10).

Jesus extends the practice of restorative justice down to his last day on earth in his physical body. There are two other men who were crucified alongside Jesus. One of them asked to be saved from his momentary suffering without acknowledging his sins. The other one agreed that he was paying the penalty for his sins, but then he turned to Jesus to ask for mercy. What he received was restorative justice; "Today you will be with me in Paradise" (Luke 23:43).

RESTORATIVE JUSTICE IN THE TWENTY-FIRST CENTURY

In America there is little interest in "restorative justice" for ex-offenders. A felony conviction in this country is actually a life sentence, because long after felons have been released from prison they have a nearly impossible time finding steady jobs. In nine states in this country their right to vote is revoked for life. There is a steady stream of people being released from America's prisons who will never be absorbed back into society because of our willingness as a nation to write the word ex-offender with indelible ink.

A *New York Times* editorial observed:

> The laws that strip ex-offenders of the right to vote across the United States are the shame of the democratic world. Of an estimated five million Americans who were barred from voting in the last presidential election (2004), a majority would have been able to vote if they had been citizens of countries like Britain, France, Germany or Australia. . . . This distinctly American bias—which extends to jobs, housing and education—keeps even law-abiding ex-offenders confined to the margins of society, where they have a notoriously difficult time building successful lives.[8]

That is, unless you are Martha Stewart, who served less than six months in prison for securities fraud and lying to a grand jury, and then received a television deal to produce a reality television show along the lines of Donald Trump's *The Apprentice*.

A TWO-TIERED SYSTEM OF JUSTICE

Federal sentencing guidelines have created a blatant discrepancy in sentencing so far as drug use in America is concerned. Under those guidelines the distinction between crack cocaine, a drug of choice by many African

Americans, and powdered cocaine, a drug of choice among whites in America, is one hundred to one. A drug dealer or someone in possession of drugs would have to possess a hundred times the amount of powdered cocaine to get the same sentence as someone who is caught in possession of a rock of crack cocaine. A report issued by the U.S. Sentencing Commission indicates that 90 percent of crack distribution offenders convicted in federal court are African American and concludes that sentences appear to be harsher and more severe for racial minorities than others as a result of the current Drug Abuse Law.[9] A *Wall Street Journal* editorial makes this disparity in sentencing crystal clear when it notes that African Americans convicted of possession of crack cocaine receive average sentences of 115 months, while whites convicted of possession of powdered cocaine receive average sentences of 77 months.[10]

This is not, by any means, an attempt to justify or condone drug abuse in America. To the contrary, drug abuse is a scourge upon our society that results in 85 percent of the crimes committed in this country—ranging from possession to theft to a wide range of crimes committed under the influence of illegal substances. However, when possession of one composition of the same drug is penalized one hundred times more severely than a different composition, and when the use of those two forms of the same drug largely follows ethnic and racial lines, the two-tiered system of justice become obvious.

The majority of people in prison in the United States are African Americans, and the vast majority of them are incarcerated on drug charges. What would the numbers look like if crack cocaine were penalized in the same way as powdered cocaine? The prison system would largely be emptied, drug treatment in lieu of conviction or incarceration would result in a sharp reduction in drug addiction, and far fewer people would be spending one to two years incarcerated on a drug charge followed by thirty to forty years labeled as ex-offenders.

BIBLICAL JUSTICE PROHIBITS EXCESSIVE PUNISHMENT

Prophetic preaching needs to reclaim the biblical notion that excessive punishment is as egregious as the crimes themselves. The law of *lex talionos* speaks about an eye for an eye and a tooth for a tooth (Exod. 21:24). This law was not solely designed to mandate punishment. It was also designed to place limits on punishment. If you lost an eye you could only seek the eye of the person who inflicted the loss upon you. You could not take a life for an eye, or two eyes for one eye. While justice needed to be enforced and people needed to be held accountable for their behavior; justice itself had to be just.

Part of biblical justice involved the Year of Jubilee: every fifty years slaves were to be freed and persons in prison were to be released. It was this concept that was being upheld in Isaiah 42:7 when the Messiah or the Servant of God would "open eyes that are blind, to free captives from prison and to release from the dungeon those who sit in darkness" (NIV). The same point is made in Isaiah 61:1, which says:

> *The spirit of God is upon me,*
> *because God has anointed me;*
> *God has sent me to bring good news to the oppressed,*
> *to bind up the brokenhearted,*
> *to proclaim liberty to the captives,*
> *and release to the prisoners.*

Of course, this is the same passage read by Jesus when he visited the synagogue in his hometown of Nazareth in Luke 4:18–19. Prophetic preaching must challenge American society regarding its treatment of prisoners and the kinds of crimes that can result in incarceration.

Justice issues do not end when the prison doors swing open, because 67 percent of all ex-offenders are rearrested within three years of their release from prison; that is according to Reginald Wilkinson, director of the Ohio Department of Rehabilitation and Corrections.[11] Investing in reentry programs can greatly reduce the likelihood of recidivism because ex-offenders will find greater assistance in making the transition back into society. Congress is considering a bill called the Second Chances Act that would use federal funds to help people make the transition to life outside of prison by providing strategic help in five areas: employment, housing, mental health, substance abuse, and support for families.

The bill took its name from comments made by George W. Bush in his 2004 State of the Union speech, in which he said:

> We know from long experience that if they can't find work—or a home or help—they are much more likely to commit crime and return to prison. . . . America is the land of second chances, and when the gates of prison open, the path ahead should lead to a better life.[12]

With two million people currently incarcerated in America, and with 650,000 persons leaving prison and returning to communities across the country each year, there is no more urgent justice issue than this. How strange that it never came up on Justice Sunday I or II.

FINANCIAL AND SOCIETAL COSTS OF WAR

It is possible that the scourge of poverty and all of its side effects could be eradicated if it were not for our nation's perennial tendency to prepare for and then wage war. The $400 billion cost of the war in Iraq eats up the money that could be used to provide job training, drug rehabilitation, more secure borders against drug trafficking and illegal immigration, higher pay for teachers and more technology for public education, or development of new industries here at home. Almost three thousand U.S. service personnel have been killed in that war and tens of thousands have been wounded both physically and mentally. No WMDs (weapons of mass destruction) were found. Conventional weapons, however, have been killing at a steady pace. Rocket propelled grenades, improvised explosive devices, and suicide bombers have claimed the lives of coalition forces and even more lives among the Iraqi people themselves.

The reasons for going to war have shifted several times since Iraq was invaded in 2003. First it was a war to find and destroy Saddam's Hussein's stockpile of nuclear, chemical, and biological weapons. We were later told that no such weapons existed there, and that we had invaded another sovereign nation that had never attacked us on the basis of "faulty intelligence." Of course, while we invaded Iraq, we never tried to invade North Korea, a country that has blatantly announced and demonstrated its nuclear development capabilities.

The war then became necessary to remove a brutal dictator named Saddam Hussein, even though that same man had been our ally when he was engaged in a war against Iran in the 1980s—a war he fought largely with weapons he acquired from the United States. The world is full of brutal dictators from the Balkans to the Andes to nations all across Africa and Asia. It seems, however, that we only choose to remove the ones who might block our access to the world's second largest reserves of oil. In the face of these inconsistencies and hypocrisies, too many Christians do their best impersonation of "hear no evil—see no evil—speak no evil" about the Bush administration and its conduct of the Iraq war. Where have all the prophets gone?

TWO WARS AT THE SAME TIME

In the 1960s, there was a similar convergence of issues of poverty on the domestic front and the costs associated with war; that time it was the war in Vietnam. In 1965, President Lyndon B. Johnson declared a war on poverty and pledged the full resources of the federal government "to end poverty in America in our lifetime." At the same time, Johnson was overseeing an escalation of the war in Vietnam at a cost of five hundred thousand dollars per day. Then, as now, the cost of war was consuming the resources that could have been directed toward a whole host of urgent social concerns. Then, as now, the war became a quagmire that failed to achieve its stated goals: the end of communism in Vietnam and democratization in Iraq.

In a famous sermon delivered at the Riverside Church in New York City entitled "A Time to Break Silence," Martin Luther King Jr. attacked the war effort and the president who was waging the war in Southeast Asia at the expense of the war on poverty here in America.[13] Hundreds of other religious leaders, including the Roman Catholic priests Daniel and Philip Berrigan and Rabbi Abraham Joshua Heschel, joined in that chorus of opposition to the war. They gave birth to an organization known as Clergy and Laity Concerned about Vietnam. They declared that American involvement in that war achieved nothing except the deaths of over fifty-eight thousand U.S. servicemen and -women. Vietnam is a communist country to this day, and the effects of the decision to ignore the war on poverty haunt this nation every day.

Will there be a similar breaking of silence when it comes to the war in Iraq? No weapons of mass destruction were found, and yet most pulpits remain silent. Osama Bin Laden has all but dropped out of focus so far as our priorities in the global war on terror are concerned; and yet most pulpits remain silent. Body bags are returning home, military funerals are being held across the country, the sound of "Taps" on a bugle and "Amazing Grace" on bagpipes is being heard over and over again. And yet most pulpits in America remain silent.

There may be a reason for this silence even in the face of this suffering and sacrifice brought on by war. It may be that many people who occupy America's pulpits believe that it is unpatriotic and un-American to criticize the war or the president. It may be that some preachers in America have allowed certain aspects of partisan politics to obscure the clear teachings of scripture about justice. This issue and the problems it poses for prophetic preaching will be the topic in the next chapter.

WHOSE DEFINITION OF JUSTICE?

The issues that I have identified as deserving attention from the pulpits of America were not randomly selected. They were not drawn from the files of the ACLU or from the platform statements of the Democratic National Convention. Every one of them came from the justice agenda of Jesus in Matthew 25:31–44: poverty, sickness, prisons, and other forms of human need. We could do a better job as a nation in resolving these problems if we heeded the advice of the prophets who long ago urged us to "beat our swords into plowshares and our spears into pruning hooks . . . and learn war no more" (Isaiah 2:4, Micah 4:3).

The reasons why we do not address these issues are many. One reason, as discussed previously, is that the very definition of justice has been hijacked by conservative, evangelical Christians. These conservative Christians obviously have no sense of the origins of the term evangelical or the aggressive justice agenda that had been attached to that term until the turn of the twentieth century. Since when has conservative evangelicalism been synonymous with the issues of abortion and human sexuality?

WHAT IS A CONSERVATIVE, EVANGELICAL CHRISTIAN?

For over four hundred years, the word evangelical described a person who was committed to the authority of scripture; the need for personal salvation through faith in Christ alone; a passion for spreading the faith to the ends of the earth; and a strong belief in the separation of church and state. The notion that someone was a "conservative" evangelical has historically implied a commitment not only to the authority of scripture, but also a belief in the infallibility or inerrancy of scripture. The struggle regarding being a conservative evangelical was more about the virgin birth of Christ than it was about abortion. It was more about the bodily resurrection of Jesus than it was about human sexuality. How has the term managed to devolve to its current understanding, and what are true evangelical preachers going to do about this distortion of the term?

Part of prophetic preaching might be to reclaim a solid and respectable Reformation word such as "evangelical." We must restore it to the historical and theological ground it once occupied and to the theological conversation about the nature of scripture and its authority within the community of faith that caused that term to be birthed. When preachers who come out of the evangelical tradition fail to speak up about the way in which that word has been twisted and distorted—as much by the news media as by those who are waging the culture war of abortion and human sexuality—they are subject to two consequences. First, they will likely be lumped together with those whom the news media calls "conservative evangelicals" whether they have bought into the culture war agenda or not. Silence will breed consent. Second, they will be turning their back on a set of issues and concerns that have given life and strength to a branch of the body of Christ since Martin Luther nailed his ninety-five theses on the door of the church in Wittenberg in 1521.

How much longer will preachers remain silent on all other justice issues except abortion and human sexuality? Those issues are not unimportant; they are simply not the length and limit of what should occupy a justice agenda in the twenty-first century. Broadening that justice agenda is the challenge for prophetic preaching as defined by James and Christine Ward in their book *Preaching from the Prophets.* They write:

> The natural inclination of the Christian community, like all religious communities, is to adapt its witness of faith to its most immediate human needs. In doing this the community always runs the risk of obscuring the wider dimensions of the gospel, particularly the wider implications of God's demand for righteousness and justice. What is needed, therefore, is preaching that recovers these wider dimensions and illuminates the ways in which the community obscures them.[14]

That is exactly what has happened to the witness of the Christian church in the twenty-first century; it has been adapted in ways that obscure the "wider dimensions of the gospel." Prophetic preaching is desperately needed to help the church recover those wider dimensions of justice and righteousness.

FOUR

FROM BIBLICAL PROPHETS TO PATRIOT PASTORS

> *Then Amos answered Amaziah, "I am no*
> *prophet, nor a prophet's son; but I am a herdsman,*
> *and a dresser of sycamore trees, and God took me*
> *from following the flock and . . . said to me,*
> *'Go, prophesy to my people Israel.' Now therefore,*
> *hear the word of God."*
>
> **—Amos 7:14–15**

Where have all the prophets gone? Why is prophetic preaching so rarely heard in the pulpits of America, and why do so many pressing issues in our society go unaddressed and unexamined by many who preach the gospel of Jesus Christ? In the previous chapters it was suggested that one obstacle was the very narrow definition of justice employed by many preachers within the conservative, evangelical Christian community, coupled with an apparent disinterest in the moral issues raised by Jesus in Matthew 25:31–44.

In this chapter another obstacle to prophetic preaching will be discussed—a dangerous form of patriotism that many of our nation's preachers have adopted. It is a patriotism that views the policies of the political party now in power and an understanding of what constitutes authentic Christian faith as being synonymous. It is difficult, if not impossible, to critique the actions and policies of elected officials and government leaders if you believe that those persons are doing God's will.

This seems to be the case for thousands of clergy across the country who have rallied to the designation of being "patriot pastors." Led by Rick Scarborough of Texas, Rod Parsley of Ohio, and D. James Kennedy of Florida, three to four thousand "patriot pastors" have been recruited in parts of the South and the Midwest to help energize the evangelical Christian vote.[1] I wonder if it occurs to these pastors that the very idea of a "patriot pastor" is an oxymoron bordering on idolatry and heresy. A pastor's allegiance should be to God and not to a political party.

A patriot pastor sounds like Amaziah, a prophet in Bethel whose ultimate allegiance was to the king of Israel and not to God (Amos 7:7). The same could be said of Hananiah, who assured King Zedekiah that nothing said by the prophet Jeremiah was true and that God was on the king's side. For whom do these patriot pastors really work? To whom are these patriot pastors ultimately accountable?

It could not possibly be the God of the Bible: the God of Amos and Micah, of Samuel and Nathan, of John the Baptist and Jesus. These were prophets and preachers who regularly stood against the political establishment of their day in the name of the God of heaven and in defense of a more just and compassionate world.

If these patriot pastors really were accountable first of all to God and the teachings of the whole Bible, their agenda would be much broader and their righteous indignation would be extended beyond their two pet projects. They would hear and respond to the cries of the homeless, the hopeless, the hungry, and the heartbroken of our society. They would oppose the human and financial waste of the war in Iraq. They would denounce social policies that see the rich getting richer as a direct result of the poor being kept as poor as possible. Where have all the prophets gone? Some have become patriot pastors.

THE CHURCH AND PARTISAN POLITICS

In the spring of 2005, the depth of this fusion between conservative, evangelical Christians and a particular political agenda was on clear display at East Waynesville Baptist Church in Waynesville, North Carolina. Nine members of that congregation were forced out of their local church as a result of their decision not to vote for George W. Bush in the 2004 presidential election. The Rev. Chan Chandler, pastor of that congregation, said that those persons needed to go because they had been "holding back the work of the Kingdom of God for way too long."[2]

The comments of Chandler, a local pastor from North Carolina, however, are greatly outweighed by the expressed political intent of U.S. Senator Sam Brownback of Kansas. While contemplating a run for the presidency in 2008, part of his strategy is to "build upon the tens of millions of dollars the Bush campaign spent to mobilize evangelical Christians." Not surprisingly, the two issues he plans to use to win over their support are his opposition to abortion rights and also to same-sex marriage. Once again the umbrella of justice seems to have room for only two issues. Brownback says "opposition to same-sex marriage has broadened the movement of social conservatism. Opposition to abortion, however, is still the movement's molten core."[3]

GEORGE W. BUSH IS NOT GOD

The first thing that must be said about this close connection between conservative, evangelical Christians and the Republican Party was stated by an editorial opinion in the solidly evangelical magazine *Christianity Today*. The editorial offered an apparent rebuke of those believed to have crossed the line of biblical and theological integrity. "George W. Bush is not God. The Declaration of Independence is not an infallible guide to Christian faith and practice. . . . The American flag is not the Cross. The Pledge of Allegiance is not the creed. God Bless America is not the doxology."[4] Stephen L. Carter, a Yale law professor also writing in *Christianity Today* warns that "reducing evangelical Christianity to a wholly owned subsidiary of any political party is a terrible thing."[5]

A SUBTLE TRANSFORMATION?

It is heartening to note that Rick Warren of the twenty-thousand-member Saddleback Church in California and author of the hugely popular *Purpose Driven Life* is beginning to focus his attention on issues of poverty and disease in Rwanda and other central African nations. In an open letter to George W. Bush that was sent to more than one hundred fifty thousand evangelicals across the country, Warren expressed his intent to begin focusing on these wider justice issues. He said, "It is a moral issue . . . and because Jesus commanded us to help the poor it is an obedience issue as well."[6]

David Brooks, writing in *The New York Times*, suggests that a subtle transformation is beginning to occur within parts of the conservative, evangelical Christian community. He says, "When I look at the evangelical community, I see a community in the midst of a transformation—branching out beyond the traditional issues of abortion and gay marriage and getting more involved in programs to help the needy."[7] Brooks offers this critique of the current direction of conservative, evangelical Christians by further saying, "We can have a culture war in this country, or we can have a war on poverty, but we can't have both."[8] This seems to be the direction in which Rick Warren is moving, and it may result in some members of the conservative, evangelical Christian community beginning to find their prophetic voice.

Brooks further suggests that there may be some disconnect and even some discontent between evangelical pastors and such groups as Focus on the Family and the Family Research Council. He says:

> Millions of evangelicals are embarrassed by the people held up by the news media as their spokesmen. Millions of evangelicals feel less represented by the culture-war centered parachurch organizations, and better represented by congregational pastors who have a broader range of interests and more passion for mobilizing volunteers to perform service. Millions of evangelicals want leaders who live the faith by serving the poor.[9]

Of course, Brooks is only speculating or perhaps overhearing some conversations to which he has access. If what he suggests is true, however, then it would be good if American society could begin hearing directly from those millions about their interest in and commitment to the poor.

Susan Page of *USA Today* reports that those millions of discontented evangelicals may be in the early stage of finding their prophetic voice. She states:

> Many evangelical Christians got involved in politics because of a single issue: abortion. But in recent years, without much notice, conservative Christians also have helped force the U.S. State Department to place a higher priority on battling religious persecution, set the stage for a cease-fire in Sudan, enact legislation aimed at reducing

prison rape in the USA and push for more funds to fight AIDS in Africa.[10]

These are positive steps that should be met with encouragement.

The National Association of Evangelicals, which represents fifty-two denominations with forty-five thousand churches and over thirty million members across the country, approved a sweeping document in October 2004 called "For the Health of the Nation: An Evangelical Call to Civic Responsibility." In addition to the issue of opposing abortion, it also seeks justice and compassion for the poor and vulnerable and calls for actions to protect the environment.[11] These too are positive steps that need to be applauded and made more widely known. Only time, however, will tell if the actions taken by the leadership of the organization can and will translate down to the grassroots level of the conservative, evangelical community.

But based upon a piece of mail I received at my home in Shaker Heights, Ohio, from a group calling itself the Center for Moral Clarity, it will not be easy for the more moderate or thoughtful voices of the conservative, evangelical community to be heard, much less heeded. The letter actually came from Rod Parsley, one of the founders of the patriot pastors. It was a form letter that was subsequently followed up by both a phone call and an e-mail message.

The letter was inviting pastors from across Ohio to a conference at Parsley's church in Columbus, Ohio, to be briefed on developments in our state concerning increasing the influence of evangelical Christians throughout the state. The briefing would be given by former governor and U.S. Senator Zell Miller of Georgia. The last time I saw Senator Miller he was on MSNBC following his address to the 2004 Republican National Convention. He was challenging MSNBC host Chris Matthews to a duel in response to a question that Matthews had raised about

Miller's comments earlier that evening. Parsley assured the readers of his letter that "God is directing our activities both on a national and a state level."

This is the theological quicksand that prevents prophetic preaching by so many in the conservative evangelical camp. How can you and why would you preach prophetically against what you believe to be the will of God? In his work with the patriot pastors Parsley organized an Ohio affiliate for the expressed purpose of recruiting two thousand patriot pastors in seven key cities in the state to play major roles in organizing their church members to vote in the May 2006 primary elections across the state. The theme of this restoration project and of the Center for Moral Clarity is forthright: *America Has a Mission to Share a Living Savior with a Dying World.*[12]

Is that really the mission of America, to share a living savior with a dying world? This may well be the mission statement of a church group or a denomination, but is that the mission of America? Such claims are not made in the Declaration of Independence or the U.S. Constitution. There is no mention of that as a mission for the nation in any of the rulings of any federal district or appellate court, much less in the rulings of the U.S. Supreme Court. The mission of America, if there is such a thing, is closer to the language of Jefferson than it is to the language of Rod Parsley—life, liberty, and the pursuit of happiness, not sharing a living savior with a dying world.

The first inherent danger in such an idea is that it exempts America itself from any critique or review. America becomes the standard or the ideal against which all other nations must be judged. As Bill McKibben has already demonstrated, however, America does not measure up very well in such comparisons.[13] The far more critical truth about this language and the men and the organization that shaped it was spoken by Rev. John Lentz of the Forest Hills Presbyterian Church in Cleveland Heights,

Ohio, after he also received a letter from Rod Parsley. Lentz writes, "This is not America's mission. . . . It is blasphemous to claim that any earthly kingdom is God's kingdom. . . . This group and those like it will stop at nothing in making America a theocracy shaped by one very limited interpretation of scripture."[14]

Where have all the prophets gone? Some have gone after a perverted political philosophy that leads them to believe that their vision of America and the reign of God on earth are synonymous. This is far more than the tolerant civil religion defined by Robert Bellah and on view in American history since Washington's first inaugural address. This is more than whether a copy of the Ten Commandments can be on display in a courtroom or a classroom. This is the pursuit of political power in order to transform culture and conduct government in accordance with the views and values of a particular religious ideology.

THE PRAYER REQUEST OF PAT ROBERTSON

Just how far some conservative, evangelical Christians would go in pursuit of their view of America became clear in the case of Pat Robertson, one of the most widely known televangelists in the world. Justice Sandra Day O'Connor retired from a lifetime appointment on the U.S. Supreme Court in order to care for her husband, who is suffering from Alzheimer's disease. Upon news of her announcement, Robertson posted a prayer on his web site and invited his 700 Club TV viewers to "pray for more vacancies on the court." He actually prayed these words on one of his programs dedicated to the confirmation of John Roberts to fill the vacancy: "Take control, God! We ask for additional vacancies on the court."

Considering the fact that all federal judges serve lifetime appointments there is only one way that God could answer the prayers of Robertson and his followers—either severe infirmity (or that of a loved one) or death. The idea of his praying for vacancies when death or disease are the only ways by which such a prayer could be answered leads one to wonder about the fact that Pat Robertson and other conservative evangelical Christians call themselves pro-life. Shall we, in the name of our Christian faith, pray for the death or debilitating condition of federal judges in order to advance whatever may be our social agenda? Where have all the prophets gone? Some are trying to advance their understanding of the realm of God by going on national television asking their listeners to pray for God to "take control" and allow members of the federal judiciary to die or become disabled.

Of course, it should not be overlooked that this is the same Pat Robertson who also suggested on his 700 Club program that CIA operatives should be dispatched to "take out" or assassinate Hugo Chavez, the president of Venezuela. This is another strange comment from someone from within the ranks of the pro-life community.

WHAT JOHN F. KENNEDY HAD IN MIND?

In 1962, President John F. Kennedy said, "God's work on earth must truly be our own." That was a quintessential utterance of American civil religion. One suspects with the rise of patriot pastors, the Center for Moral Clarity, the prayer requests of Pat Robertson, and other expressions of the conservative, evangelical community that Kennedy's words have been reworked. Now it seems we live in a country where patriot pastors believe and say, "Our work on earth is truly God's will." That leaves no room for those pastors to be critiqued and even less reason for them to critique the nation. Where have all the prophets gone?

WHAT DOES JUSTICE LOOK LIKE?

Prophetic preaching should call the church of Jesus Christ to a form of justice that is vastly more inclusive than the issues of abortion or human sexuality. It should be inclusive not only in terms of the sheer number of such issues, but inclusive also in terms of the number of people who are confronted by the need for biblical justice every day. In the Old Testament, there is repeated concern for widows, orphans, and strangers in the land (Deut. 14:29, Isa. 1:17–23, Jer. 7:6, Hos. 14:3, Zech. 7:10, Mal. 3:5). In Matthew 25:31–44, Jesus clearly sets forth the issues of greatest concern to him, issues by which it will be determined who will be admitted into the God's realm: "I was hungry and you fed me, I was thirsty and you gave me drink, I was naked and you clothed me, I was sick and you cared for me, I was in prison and you came to see me." That is the direction in which Rick Warren is trying to lead his conservative evangelical colleagues, and that is clearly the direction in which scripture is pointing. Anything less than this falls grievously short of the will of God.

In the March 22, 2005, issue of *The Christian Century,* an editorial appears under the heading of "Where's the Compassion?" It asserts:

> While biblical justice included charity for the needy, it also included means to even the playing field between rich and poor—affirmative action for those left out or left behind—such as the sabbatical year that liberated slaves and forgave debts. And the prophets castigated commercial practices that took advantage of the people already suffering[15]

These are some of the issues of justice that are consistently left out when "Justice Sundays" are held. These are the issues and the people caught up in them that are at the heart of prophetic preaching. It is past time for these concerns to be voiced and for those people who have fallen victim to these issues to find an advocate in the pulpits of America.

PATRIOT PASTORS MUST BECOME PROPHETS

It is most unlikely that the voice of prophetic preaching will echo widely throughout this country so long as preachers are more interested in being "patriot pastors" than they are in being prophets who, like Isaiah, are prepared to "shout out, do not hold back!" (Isa. 58:1). If a trip to the White House and a photo opportunity with a government official is all that is needed to silence the voice of protest and advocacy in America, then very little prophetic preaching will be heard. If faith-based funding can be offered and pastors become mute when those who extended the grant later behave immorally, it is little wonder that prophetic preaching is so rarely heard in America.

Of course, that was not the case when King Ahab confronted the prophet Elijah and accused him of being "the troubler of Israel." Rather than seek favor with the king or federal funding from the government, Elijah answered back and told Ahab, "I have not troubled Israel; but you have, and your father's house, because you have forsaken the commandments of God and followed the Baals" (1 Kings 18:17–18). This was not the case when the prophet Nathan confronted King David following the king's adulterous and murderous encounter with Bathsheba and Uzziah. The prophet did not look the other way or assure the king that God did not mind what had happened. Nathan stood toe to toe with King David and told him "You are the man!" (2 Sam. 12:7). These men were not "patriot pastors"; they were prophets of God.

Samuel was no "patriot pastor" when he confronted King Saul about his disobedience regarding the battle with Agag and the Amalekites, telling him that God was grieved that he had ever chosen Saul to be the king. God spoke to Samuel with these words, "I regret that I made Saul king, for he has turned back from following me, and has not carried out my commands" (1 Sam. 15:11). Hanani was no "patriot pastor" when he confronted King Asa about his willingness to put his faith in a treaty with the king of Arum rather than putting his faith in God. He told the king, "You have done foolishly in this; for from now on you will have wars" (2 Chron. 16:7–9).

John the Baptist was no "patriot pastor" when he confronted King Herod Antipas for breaking the law of Moses and marrying the wife of his brother Philip while his brother was still alive (Matt. 14:3). Jesus was no "patriot pastor" when he stood before the Sanhedrin and Pontius Pilate and declared himself to be the Son of God (Matt. 26:64, Mark 14:62, Luke 22:70) and the king of the Jews (John 18:37). Peter and John were not "patriot pastors" when, having been ordered by the Sanhedrin never again to speak openly about Jesus, they answered by saying, "Whether it is right in God's sight to listen to you rather than to God, you must judge; for we cannot keep from speaking about what we have seen and heard" (Acts 4:19–20).

If prophetic preaching is to be heard in proportion to the challenges and conditions that currently confront this country, preachers will have to find the courage and the boldness to stand up to and speak out against the people and policies responsible for those conditions. Preachers will have to understand that "God Bless America" is a patriotic tune and not a theological mandate. "In God We Trust" may be engraved upon our nation's currency, but there is no evidence that those words have been etched upon the hearts of our nation's leaders. How long will America's preachers go limping between two opinions? Are we "patriot pastors" or are we preachers of the gospel with a broad definition of justice and a deep sense of compassion who feel at liberty to say to our own government, "This is what God says?"

T. D. JAKES AND GEORGE W. BUSH

All preachers can learn a lesson about prophetic preaching simply by noting the words and timing of Bishop T. D. Jakes, founder and pastor of the Potter's House in Dallas, Texas. Bishop Jakes was asked to preach at a prayer service at the National Cathedral in Washington, D.C., in the wake of Hurricane Katrina. With the president of the United States seated in the front row, Jakes did not hold back his prophetic message. He could have asked God's blessings on those who had been affected. He could have asked God to grant wisdom to the president as he faced the days ahead. To his credit, he did neither of those two "priestly" tasks. Instead, he spoke a prophetic word to the president, to the dignitaries gathered in that cathedral, and to the whole nation that was glued to television screens watching the events in New Orleans and other places. He said:

> Restoration is more than observation. It is more than looking from the safety of our television into the lives of other people, and assessing their situation from the comfort of our own luxuries and lives. . . . This can no longer be a nation that overlooks the poor and the suffering and continues past the ghetto on our way to the Mardi Gras.[16]

Amen, Bishop Jakes. Amen!

FIVE

WHEN PROPHETIC PREACHING GIVES WAY TO PRAISE

Take away from me the noise of your songs;
I will not listen to the melody of your harps.
But let justice roll down like waters, and
righteousness like an everflowing stream.

—Amos 5:23–24

It is the central hypothesis of this book that prophetic preaching in the pulpits of churches in America has been hushed, hindered, and hijacked by preachers who have gone off in service to other gods. In the previous chapter, a case was made for the negative impact of patriot pastors on the work of prophetic preaching. In that instance, attention was directed primarily, though not exclusively to white, conservative, evangelical Christians.

In this chapter, the next obstacle to be discussed will be praise and worship. There is a growing tendency to be so centered on the celebration of the faith in praise and worship that it leaves no time for and places little, if any, emphasis on the issues of justice and righteousness.

PROPHETIC PREACHING IS MISSING

The crisis is not simply in the pulpits of local churches across the country; the situation is equally dire so far as pastors' conferences, denominational conventions, and preaching journals and magazines are concerned. The burning concerns of prophetic preaching are almost entirely absent. There is a deafening silence on such matters as society's care for "the least of these"; the sovereignty of God over the whole creation and not just over America; the lingering problem of racism and the festering problem of sexism; the economic and human costs of war and the affect that it has on domestic programs; and many other moral and ethical demands that are part of the life of a disciple of Jesus Christ.

Instead, there is a constant call to "praise God" that is seldom, if ever, followed up with a challenge to serve God in tangible ways that are of benefit to our brothers and sisters, to our neighbors and friends, or to the widows, orphans, and strangers who are so constantly referenced in the Bible. If you listen to sermons on religious television channels, on station after station, day after day, on one program after another, you will hear this theme of praise severed from the prophetic message.

Whether you listen to the predominantly African American preachers on the WORD Network or the predominantly white preachers on the Trinity Broadcasting Network, the message is the same. People are being invited into a celebration of their faith during worship service without any corresponding challenge to live out their faith in the face of social injustice. It was exactly that kind of religious practice that was so strongly condemned by the prophet Amos as he confronted the people of Israel for offering God their songs but not their service, their music but not their moral outrage over needless human suffering, and their harps that lift music up to God but not their outstretched hands reaching to lift up a fallen brother or sister.

Another reason for the decline in prophetic preaching in America is the rise of preachers whose primary aim is the emotional release that many Christians experience on Sunday morning. Regretfully, this is not the empathetic response that should come when hearts made tender by the gospel of Jesus Christ see the pain and suffering that marks our nation and our world. Shouting, "Amen!" and crying out, "Hallelujah!" does not remove the drug trafficking that plagues our society. Having a "Holy Ghost good time" does not prevent one job from being downsized or outsourced or lost as a result of corporate corruption or mismanagement. "Praising God" as an end in itself, without political advocacy or public protest, will not bring our troops home from Afghanistan or Iraq or provide them with a rational reason for being there in the first place.

TELEVANGELISTS: PART OF THE PROBLEM?

One of the reasons why prophetic preaching has given way to praise may be the prominence and pervasiveness of certain televangelists who never come close to offering a serious critique either of the church or of society as a whole. The entire nation seems to have fallen in love with Joel Osteen of Houston, Texas, who has just moved his twenty-five-thousand-member congregation into the sixteen-thousand-seat Compaq Center. This massive facility was the former home to the Houston Rockets basketball team. After $95 million in renovations, the Lakewood Church has two waterfalls but does not display a cross, the central symbol of the Christian faith.

It is little wonder that there is no cross, because in Osteen's preaching, no cross is necessary—only positive thinking. He was recently quoted as saying, "It's about giving hope, giving encouragement. . . . For so long, people have been beat down, just by life in general. God is good, he's for you. You can be happy."[1] Nothing was said, however, about the conditions and circumstances that caused people to be beaten down in the first place, or about how we as followers of Jesus Christ can and should respond to those problems. All the work is left to God, and all that is required of believers is that they receive the blessings that God is waiting to give them.

Osteen's congregation is a charismatic church where worshippers are likely to be "slain in the spirit," but not at all likely to be challenged concerning any of the issues of the day. John Leland of *The New York Times* notes that "if not for the religious references, Mr. Osteen's sermons on topics like procrastination, submitting to authority, and staying positive could be secular motivational speeches.[2] Attendees may find themselves on the floor while speaking in tongues, but they are not likely to encounter any serious theological question or ethical dilemma. Osteen himself says, "I don't get deep and theological"[3] Lynn Mitchell, director of religious studies at the University of Houston says, "The idea of suffering as a Christian virtue is not a part of his worldview. Some call it Christianity Lite—you get all of the benefits but don't pay attention to the fact that Jesus called for suffering. He doesn't tackle many of the problems of the world."[4] One critic refers to Osteen's preaching as "cotton candy theology."[5]

MEGACHURCHES WITH A MINI GOSPEL?

There is nothing wrong with a megachurch so long as its foundations are not rooted in a minigospel, but that is exactly what seems to be happening. There is ample emphasis on praise and worship and celebration and feeling good; however, there is scarcely a word about duty or discipleship or self-denial for the sake of others. Such churches need an immediate and intense exposure to Amos 5:23–24 where

God announces that songs of praise and shouts of celebration in worship are unacceptable if they are not accompanied by works of justice and righteousness. The same point is made in Micah 6:6–8 where God announces no interest in expensive sacrifices as signs of worship and devotion. Instead, God wants us to "do justice, and to love kindness, and to walk humbly with your God."

There is no doubt that God is deserving of praise. The point of this chapter is not to argue that people should not praise God. Psalm 150 is wholeheartedly endorsed: "Let everything that breathes praise God!" Whether praise is invited during a time of song and prayer or as a response to some part of a sermon, praise is a good thing. I concur with the verse that says, "It is good to give thanks to God, to sing praises to your name, O Most High"(Psa. 92:1).The question at hand is whether the God who is worthy of being praised is also worthy and deserving of being obeyed. Isn't this that same God who calls upon us to serve God by working for a more just and peaceful and humane social order?

SOMETIMES ONLY PRAISE WILL DO

Praise is especially important and appropriate in those instances when God has brought people through some challenging and dangerous season in their lives. When someone has survived cancer, divorce, unemployment, or the flood waters of the Gulf Coast after Hurricane Katrina, they may want to shout out, *"Thank you, Jesus!"* When people's lives are miraculously spared following an accident of one type or another, it would not be surprising to hear them exclaim, *"God, I praise you!"* There is a song that says:

> *For every mountain you brought me over,*
> *For every trial you brought me through . . .*
> *For this I give you praise.*[6]

There are also seasons of joy and celebration when praise is appropriate. When a child is born, praise makes sense. When the first person in the family to graduate from college walks across the stage to receive a diploma, praise makes sense. This person carries the pride and sense of achievement of the forbearers to whom the door of higher education had been firmly closed either because of cost or color. Somebody in the audience is going to shout out, "Praise God!"

Even death can be an occasion when praise is appropriate. I can recall as a child attending a service held annually at our church on New Year's Eve. At about 11:45 P.M., the pastor would invite the congregation to form a circle along the walls of the sanctuary while the lights were dimmed. For the next few minutes, he would call off the names of people from within that congregation who died during that past year. As each name was called, someone from within that sanctuary could be heard crying out, "Thank you, Jesus!"

In my youth, I misunderstood that sequence of events and thought the person still alive was celebrating the fact that someone was dead. As I learned later on, that was precisely the wrong conclusion. Those people who were praising God were not happy because their loved ones were dead, they were rejoicing because their faith assured them that their loved ones were absent from the body and present with God (2 Cor. 5:6–8). Life on earth was over, but eternal life with God had just begun. It was that kind of faith that has allowed Christians to face death with such firm resolve for two millenia. There are many moments in the life of a Christian and in the liturgy and order of worship of a congregation when praise is the most important thing that can be done.

A BALANCE BETWEEN PRAISE AND WORSHIP

What is being called for is not the elimination of praise from the life of the believer, but rather a balance in the life of every church and every believer between times of praise and worship and times when our focus is directed to the justice agenda raised by Jesus. As was the case with the issue of patriot pastors and conservative evangelical Christians who draw too close a link between the Christian faith and partisan politics, the words of Jesus in Matthew 25:31–44 also pose a challenge for those whose gospel is limited solely or even primarily to the practice of praise. Jesus says that what interests him most is that his disciples will respond to those who are hungry, thirsty, naked, sick, or imprisoned. "Giving God some praise" may make for a spirited worship service, but it does not necessarily translate into a life that is pleasing and acceptable to God. In Matthew 7:21 and Luke 6:46 Jesus warns people against saying "Lord, Lord" while not doing God's will. And Jesus indicates his will as directly as possible when he says in Matthew 22:37–40:

> "You shall love your Sovereign God with all your heart, and with all your soul, and with all your mind." This is the greatest and first commandment. And a second is like it: "You shall love your neighbor as yourself." On these two commandments hang all the law and the prophets.

Let us suppose that praise and worship can comfortably fall under the commandment to love God with all our heart, soul, and mind. Throwing our hearts and souls into acts of praise and worship may be one of the ways that we demonstrate how much we love God.

This leaves out, however, the second part of the statement—to love our neighbor as we love ourselves—the part that calls us away from praising God in the sanctuary toward caring for our neighbor as we encounter our neighbors throughout the community and the society. What Amos and Micah were calling for was not an end to acts of praise worship, but the striking of a balance so that the deeds of justice and righteousness are not overlooked or ignored while Christians are busy "having a high time in the house of God."

ENTER TO WORSHIP—DEPART TO SERVE

Many congregations use worship bulletins where this balance is reinforced in print every Sunday morning: "Enter to worship—Depart to serve." On the way in, the emphasis is on praise and worship and giving glory to God. There is time for hymns and other songs and also time for prayers and testimonies. At the end of the worship service, however, the congregation must be challenged as to how they should live their lives and how they should engage their neighbor and the wider society. In other words, the problem is not that people are praising God and lifting holy hands in the sanctuary. The problem arises when nothing in the service—especially in the sermon—challenges people to move beyond worship to service and self-sacrifice.

Prophetic preaching is designed to motivate people to move beyond lifting up holy hands and begin to extend helping hands to those Jesus describes in Matthew 25 as "the least of these." It is not a matter of one over the other, nor is it a matter of one being more important than the other. Rather, it is a matter of seeing that one is really impossible without the other. We cannot serve God in this world of evil and corruption as we should unless we have a sense of the glory and greatness of God that is perfected in times of praise and worship. Similarly, we cannot sing "What a mighty God we serve" and then fail or refuse to work to establish a more humane and just society in the name of that mighty God.

PRAISE NOT AN END IN ITSELF

In his book *The Ministry of Music in the Black Church*, J. Wendell Mapson Jr. makes some observations about the evolution of music in the life of the black church that helps to point out the danger that arises when praise is separated from the continuing work of discipleship and service. He writes:

> Increasingly, music in the black church has been separated from its theological and historical underpinnings. Instead of serving theology as a legitimate response to God and telling the story of hardship, disappointment, and hope, music in the black church has become, in many instances, an end in itself. This often fosters the goal of entertainment rather than the goal of ushering people into the very presence of the Almighty and sending them forth to serve.[7]

The danger of praise and worship fostering a goal of entertainment is a real danger in many churches today. The theological question that needs to be engaged is whether or not praise and worship should be viewed as ends in themselves, or if they are better viewed as an inseparable component of a cycle of rituals or sacred acts that should always include some challenge to action beyond the time of praise and worship themselves. Praise and worship are useful and important acts, but what do they lead to once the worship service is over?

PRAISE WITHOUT PROPHETIC PREACHING IS CHEAP GRACE

Preachers and people who settle for a spiritual diet limited to praise and worship are offering up and operating on a gospel of cheap grace. In their theology, Jesus Christ has done all the work on the cross or will continue to provide for the needy and those who turn to him in prayer. For that provision, they give thanks to God. Such a gospel requires no sacrifice, it demands no obedience, and it calls for no engagement with what is happening in the lives of people outside the doors of the church or across the country or around the world. People may be asked to tithe a portion of their income to support the ministries of their church, but they may never be called upon to serve a hot meal to a homeless person or visit the inmates in the nearest correctional center or attend an outdoor vigil in front of the scene of yet another senseless murder in our violent and gun-crazed society.

It would make no sense to call for the elimination of praise and worship in the life of the Christian because praise and worship only involve an hour or two on those Sundays when worshippers gather in the sanctuary. The question is: "What's next during the 166 hours that will intervene until the worshippers meet together again? The answer is that worship and praise are preparation for and refreshment from the work of ministry and service that ought to follow the benediction. Enter to worship— Depart to serve.

NOT A NEW PROBLEM

In a biography of the renowned Baptist preacher Clarence Lavaughn (C. L.) Franklin entitled *Singing the Lord's Song,* reference is made to research that was conducted in Memphis, Tennessee, in 1940 during the time when Franklin was a pastor in that city. It was conducted by Ralph Bunche, who would later work for the United Nations and become the first African American to win the Nobel Peace Prize. Bunche noted that there were 375 churches in Memphis, and of that number 213 were African American congregations. Bunche said, "Those churches and their pastors had no voice when it came to the issues that confronted blacks in Memphis."[8] Bunche continued:

> The Negro preachers of Memphis as a whole have avoided social questions. They have preached thunder and lightning, fire and brimstone, Moses out of the bulrushes, but about the economic and political exploitation of local blacks, they have remained silent.[9]

Sadly, if Bunche were to have done similar research in any other city that houses a significant black population, in every decade since the 1940s he would probably come to the same conclusion. Far too many black churches remain mute in the face of social issues. They are inactive or unresponsive when the call to action is sounded to address or correct social ills.

Across the country during the height of the civil rights movement of the 1950s and 1960s, most African American pastors and churches remained uninvolved. They continued to hold church services and prayer meetings, but they did not open their doors, their budgets, or their hearts to the protests and demonstrations that were in pursuit of a more just society. Clarence James, author of "Lost Generation or Left Generation?" offers a description of this problem that persists to the present day. He says:

> The trouble with today's clergy is there are too many priests and not enough prophets. The priests are the servants of the privileged, criticizing little crimes at the bottom while ignoring those at the top. The prophets remind the rulers they are not exempt from the laws of God, but the priests are blinded by wealth and power.[10]

Is it possible that many preachers and pastors who could speak a prophetic word in the face of all that confronts our nation and our world are really more concerned about personal comfort and the good graces of those who pay their salaries and donate toward the construction of their megachurches?

A REMINDER OF WHAT IS WRONG

In my book *Preaching to the Black Middle Class*, I try to make this point through the use of Luke 16:19–31, the parable of the rich man and Lazarus. Earlier in my career,

I interpreted that passage using a racial motif, identifying poor Lazarus as the impoverished and neglected black community while the rich man was, of course, white society that lived well and cared little for the black neighbor just outside its door. That was an inaccurate reading of that text because both Lazarus and the rich man were Jews. What divided them was not color or ethnicity; what divided them was class or income.[11]

There are black churches throughout America located in neighborhoods that resemble bombed-out war zones. They are infested with drugs, alcoholism, HIV/AIDS, prostitution, and domestic violence. The poverty rates among school age children approach 65 percent. More often than not there is little if any interaction between those black congregations and the people and/or the problems that reside just outside the doors of the church buildings.

Worship service occurs on Sunday morning and perhaps again on Wednesday night; but not much else takes place during the week. Many of the churches sit idle and unused. The buildings are locked most of the time. The congregation, most of whom drive to the church from outlying neighborhoods and from the surrounding suburbs, have no interest or investment in the neighborhood, its people, or their problems. They just come to church "to get their praise on" and then get back in their cars and go home.

The people in those churches do not notice Lazarus as he sits just outside the door. They do not see the bleary-eyed woman who has walked the street all night long turning tricks for a pimp who beats her if she does not bring him enough money. They do not see posted signs declaring a certain house closed because it had become a "shooting gallery" for drug users. They see but do not engage the young men with their pants sagging and their tee shirts below their knees who have no place to go and nothing to do. They do not see the teenage mother with her third child or the police brutality that so often follows an incident of "driving while black."

They go to church to praise God, but they either will not notice or will not engage the issues of justice and righteousness that exist all around them every Sunday morning. What is needed is a prophetic critique that confronts the society that allows such conditions to persist as well as a prophetic critique of any local church or any Christian denomination that knows such problems exist but says and does nothing to impact or alleviate the problems. Such a critique, however, is most unlikely in churches that are so focused on praise and worship that they give no thought to and make no provision for issues of justice and righteousness and peace. In such cases, it is the churches themselves that need the challenge of a prophetic critique.

BALANCING PRAISE WITH PROPHETIC PREACHING

One way for preachers to assist people in finding the balance between praise and the performance of justice and righteousness comes from a homiletic principle dealing with sermon outcomes. In his book *The Making of the Sermon*, Robert McCracken, who followed Harry Emerson Fosdick as pastor of Riverside Church in New York City, made reference to four possible outcomes from a sermon, which he called "kindling the mind, energizing the will, disturbing the conscience, and stirring the heart."[12] The balance between praise and worship on the one hand and prophetic preaching on the other hand involves the principles of disturbing the conscience and stirring the heart. The first two principles, however, should first be reviewed.

KINDLE THE MIND

To kindle the mind should be viewed as an approach to a controversial sermon on a complex topic or text. The primary goal of a sermon using this principle is to encourage people to think about that topic for the first time or to challenge them to rethink views they had formerly held. The preacher's task is to provide the information for both sides of an issue, insert the relevant biblical background and theological focus, then leave it up to the listeners to think about what has been said and begin to make up their minds.

ENERGIZE THE WILL

To energize the will is to move people beyond the thinking stage and motivate them to take action in a certain arena. Whether the issue is race relations, women in ministry, issues of war and peace, an environmental concern, or some ecumenical or interfaith matter, the goal of this sermon is to persuade people to act. It is very possible that one or more sermons will previously have been preached that allowed for some kindling of the mind. Now the preacher's job is to energize the will and give people the motivation and the methodology to take the necessary action.

DISTURB THE CONSCIENCE

So far as prophetic preaching in balance with praise and worship is concerned, the last two principles offer the most guidance. To disturb the conscience is to intentionally set before the people the issues of sin, confession, repentance, and restoration. Romans 3:23 remains true: "All have sinned and fall short of the glory of God." Romans 7:18b–19 remains true: "I can will what is right but I cannot do it. For I do not do the good I want, but the evil I do not want is what I do." The task of prophetic preaching, whether it is done in the context of a local church or in a farther reaching format, is to set before people those ways in which we/they are not doing the good they should be doing. Just as importantly, prophetic preaching must seek to name the evils we/they are doing and call people to repentance.

It is impossible to avoid this third principle of disturbing the conscience if you take seriously the lessons of scripture. When Nathan confronted David concerning the king's sins in the Bathsheba episode, the prophet's intention was to disturb the conscience of the king. When Hosea confronted Israel about that nation's "adulterous affair" with idols and false gods, the prophet's goal was to disturb the conscience. When both John the Baptist in Mark 1:4 and Jesus in Mark 1:15 preached their first sermons, both of them preached about the need for repentance. Their goal was to disturb the conscience.

It is imperative that preachers learn this lesson if we are to be faithful to God and useful to those to whom we preach. In Acts 20:27, as his ministry is coming to an end, Paul says, "I have not hesitated to proclaim to you the whole will of God" (NIV). This cannot be done unless and until some of our sermons have disturbing the conscience as their intended goal. As the prophet Ezekiel was told both in 3:18–19 and again in 33:7–9, there is a consequence that falls to the preacher who does not speak truth to people who could end up saving their lives and securing their souls. People may not listen to us when we preach such sermons, and they may choose to hear us and then simply ignore everything they heard. Their decision is between them and God. If, however, we fail to say something simply because it is unpleasant or unpopular, then both the people and the preacher will face God's judgment together.

In Ezekiel 18, attention is given to the justice issues that should concern us when we preach a prophetic critique. The prophet says:

> If a man is righteous and does what is lawful and right—if he does not eat upon the mountains or lift up his eyes to the idols of the house of Israel, does not defile his neighbor's wife or approach a

woman during her menstrual period, does not oppress anyone, but restores to the debtor his
pledge, commits no robbery, gives his bread to
the hungry and covers the naked with a garment,
does not take advance or accrued interest, with-
holds his hand from iniquity, executes true justice
between contending parties, follows my statues,
and is careful to observe my ordinances, acting
faithfully—such a one is righteous; he shall surely
live, says your Sovereign God. (Ezek. 18:5–9)

If at any point the people to whom we preach are
falling short of this standard of justice and righteousness,
it is our responsibility to disturb the conscience and say,
"This is what God says." If we fail to do so, the people will
still face the consequences of their unjust and unright-
eous behavior, but God will hold us responsible for their
blood (Ezek. 3:18).

STIR THE HEART

Having given equal and adequate attention to a sermon
schedule that rotates between the first three principles,
including disturbing the conscience, there is still ample
opportunity for sermons designed to lead people in praise
and thanksgiving. This is the primary goal of sermons designed to stir the heart. Here is where such themes as the
love, grace, mercy, and glory of God can be addressed.
Here is where assurance can be given to people in times
of sickness or distress or in the face of death: "Even
though I walk through the darkest valley, I fear no evil; for
you are with me . . ." (Psa. 23:4a).

It is appropriate to design worship services and the
sermons that will be preached at those services around
themes that generate shouts of "Glory, hallelujah!" "For
the one who is in you is greater than the one who is in the
world" (1 John 4:4). Glory, hallelujah! "The steadfast love

of God never ceases, his mercies never come to an end. They are new every morning" (Lam. 3:22–23). Praise God! "For I am convinced . . . nor anything else in all creation, will be able to separate us from the love of God in Christ Jesus our Sovereign" (Rom. 8:38–9). Thank you, Jesus!

BALANCE AND ROTATION OF THEMES

The goal of this chapter is not to eliminate praise and worship from the life of the Christian or the life of the congregation. To the contrary, those are precious and sacred moments when believers stand in the presence of "the only God our savior," to whom "through Jesus Christ our Sovereign, be glory, majesty, power, and authority . . ." (Jude 25). What is being sought is a balance that is missing from so many churches and from so many pulpits across America. Simply by moving from kindling the mind to energizing the will to disturbing the conscience to stirring the heart, a preacher can be sure that God is being praised on the one hand and is also being served and obeyed on the other hand.

The system is proven and tested and is now awaiting any and all preachers who have the courage, the convictions, and the compassion to call the church's attention to the "least of these" in our society. The rotation is reliable and will eventually bring the preacher to the moment when truth must be spoken to power about the policies and practices that continue to result in an unjust social order where the rich get richer and the poor get poorer. Stirring the heart is a good thing to do, but never to the exclusion of those texts and topics that result in disturbing the conscience.

PROTEST AND PRAISE IN THE CIVIL RIGHTS ERA

There is no better example of the balance between prophetic preaching and praise and worship than what was widely experienced during the civil rights movement of the 1950s and 1960s. Those who shared in that movement can still feel the power and energy of the worship services that were held in hot and crowded churches. People prayed and sang and preached with a fervor unmatched by any Pentecostal or charismatic assembly.

The worship service, however, was never viewed as an end in itself. Rather, it was viewed as a bridge over troubled waters as the people were returning from or heading toward an encounter with racism, segregation, hatred, and violence. There was no doubt that the people "entered to worship." It was equally clear, however, that they would soon "depart to serve." The energy of the worship made the times of service possible, and the rigors and risks of the service made the worship necessary. Neither of those two aspects of the civil rights movement would have made any sense without the other. Protest and praise, "Thank you, Jesus" and "Freedom now," were inseparably tied together.

Those who remember that era feel more intensely the absence of any such balance in church life today. When a passionate time of praise and worship is disconnected from a disciplined and determined time of service and even sacrifice in the name of God, the worship itself becomes invalid and inauthentic. People enter to worship but they depart to brunch or a round of golf or an afternoon in front of the television with the NFL or NBA or their favorite movie. The remainder of the week is occupied with the regular routines of life. At no point do people feel the need to speak up about war and peace, bias and discrimination, the increase in such pain indices as poverty, incarceration, teen and out-of-wedlock birth, HIV/AIDS infection rates, drug and alcohol abuse, failing public schools in inner cities, unemployment and the outsourcing of jobs, and/or domestic violence and divorce.

PRAISE AND JUSTICE IN THE BIBLICAL PROPHETS

All of the above listed topics deserve and demand a prophetic critique from the believing community. Rarely, if ever, does such a critique occur because too many people—and the preachers who speak to them—have little interest in doing anything faith-related beyond lifting up holy hands and "getting their praise on." The believing community, therefore, is deserving of a prophetic critique for its unwillingness to maintain the balance between personal piety and personal responsibility for performing works of justice and righteousness.

It really is no different than it was in the days of Amos, Micah, Hosea, and Isaiah. In the eighth century B.C.E., prophets of the Old Testament voiced God's displeasure with people who disconnected their personal piety from any personal responsibility for giving voice and shape to a more just social order.

For I desire steadfast love and not sacrifice,
the knowledge of God rather than burnt offerings.
    (Hos. 6:6)

I hate, I despise your festivals. . . .
Take away from me the noise of your songs; . . .
But let justice roll down like waters,
and righteousness like an everflowing stream.
    (Amos 5:21–24)

He has told you, O mortal, what is good;
And what does the LORD require of you
but to do justice, and to love kindness,
and to walk humbly with your God?
    (Mic. 6:8)

Is not this the fast that I choose:
to loose the bonds of injustice, to undo the thongs of the yoke,
to let the oppressed go free, and to break every yoke?

> *It is not to share your bread with the hungry,*
> *and bring the homeless poor into your house;*
> *when you see the naked, to cover them,*
> *and not to hide yourself from your own kin?*
>   (Isa. 58:6–7)

AWAKEN PASSIVE CHRISTIANS

In a generation when more and more believers seem to be content with praise and worship to the exclusion of justice and righteousness, the task of the preacher is to awaken the church. It must be awakened to its role and responsibility as a herald of the justice agenda of the realm of God. The problem that must be overcome to establish the needed balance is quoted by James Cone in an essay entitled "The Pastor as Servant." This well-stated document was circulated at a poor people's rally in Albuquerque, New Mexico. It states:

> *I was hungry*
> *And you formed a humanities club*
> *And you discussed my hunger.*
> *Thank you.*
>
> *I was imprisoned*
> *And you crept off quietly*
> *To your chapel in the cellar*
> *And prayed for my release.*
>
> *I was sick*
> *And you knelt and thanked God*
> *For your health.*
>
> *I was homeless*
> *And you preached to me*
> *Of the spiritual shelter of the love of God.*
>
> *I was lonely*
> *And you left me alone*

To pray for me.
You seem so holy;
So close to God.

But I'm still very hungry
And lonely
And cold.

So where have your prayers gone?
What have they done?
What does it profit a man
To page through his book of prayers
When the rest of the world is crying for his help?[13]

SIX

From Prophets to Profits: Reflections on the Prosperity Gospel

Her leaders judge for a bribe,
her priests teach for a price, and her prophets
tell fortunes for money.

—Micah 3:11 (NIV)

Where have all the prophets gone? The absence of prophetic preaching in pulpits across America has so far been considered from three perspectives.

The first obstacle to prophetic preaching is the emergence of a narrow definition of justice. This definition only involves the issues of abortion and various aspects of human sexuality over all other issues confronting our nation and our world. The second obstacle is the loss of identity by preachers who are more interested in being "patriot pastors," who blindly sing "God Bless America," rather than filling the role of biblical prophets who serve a sovereign God who has "the whole world in his hands." The third obstacle is praise and worship that is largely devoid of any references to justice and righteousness. Preachers who promote this are more focused on inviting believers to lift up holy hands than they are in urging those same believers to extend helping hands to those in need. At the turn of the twenty-first century, these three observations point to serious distortions of the preaching task, which distract attention away from the texts and themes that should be considered in preaching in America.

In this chapter, we look at a fourth reason for the decline of prophetic preaching—the emergence of "prosperity theology." This approach to preaching concentrates on a formula that seems to promise wealth and prosperity to those who follow the prescribed principles. Once again, it seems, the issues of justice and righteousness have taken a back seat in many pulpits across America while the issues of dollars and cents have assumed the central role. This approach to preaching is based upon references to a variety of passages that seem to promise great blessings to those who have enough faith. More often than not, prosperity preachers provide little if any accurate exegesis of those biblical texts. The scriptures are used only as a platform from which the promises of health and wealth are declared.

THE ABUNDANT LIFE OR THE "GOOD LIFE"?

The abundant life that Jesus referred to seems to have lost out to John Locke's concept of "the good life." In America, there has always been a preoccupation with wealth and prosperity. America has always been idealized as a land of plenty. America was the place where a person could start out with nothing and end up a millionaire. Countless generations of people have immigrated to this country in search of that dream. Tens of millions of Africans were forcibly brought to this country to become the tools by which others could pursue this dream of wealth and prosperity. America was born out of the idea of "the good life" as defined by John Locke, who spoke about "life, liberty, and the pursuit of property."[1] This was transformed by Thomas Jefferson into the central credo of our nation's Declaration of Independence: "Life, liberty, and the pursuit of happiness."

The pursuit of happiness has almost always been presented as the pursuit of prosperity or wealth, and that pursuit has consumed this nation from its inception. The pursuit of happiness sometimes sends people off in search of sensual pleasures. Other times, it is a quest for the latest thrill or an ever more intense "high" brought on either from some illegal drug or the abuse of alcohol. So desperate have people become for happiness, pleasure, thrills, and highs that, as I heard one preacher say about himself, he will "try anything that will offer a little bit of peace for a short period of time." The problem with the good life and the pursuit of happiness is that there is never a moment when one has "arrived" at that point. The pursuit of happiness is an endless quest, and final attainment of the good life always seems to be a new house or another car. Every television commercial and newspaper advertisement points toward the pursuit of happiness. If you drive the right car you will achieve happiness. If you wear the right designer labels you will achieve happiness. If you can manage to live in a certain house or in a certain neighborhood, you will achieve happiness.

People strive for happiness and prosperity at every turn. They put their children in certain schools because they think that by doing so they will increase their children's chances of living a better life. People make their career choices with less interest in how that decision might impact society for better or for worse, and with more focus on how they can earn the most money and live the best possible life. This book is not intended to reverse the centuries of aspiration in American society, although such a reverse is desperately needed.

This aspiration for wealth and prosperity has been the driving force in most of the human suffering that this nation has experienced. It was the force behind slavery, child labor, and the downsizing and outsourcing of jobs to other places in the world where lower wages can be paid and where fewer environmental rules must be followed. Our reckless pursuit of happiness has also resulted in enormous suffering in other nations. America has milked other societies for their mineral and human resources. These injustices have allowed us to live the good life about which most Americans dream, a life in which the global exploited masses cannot and were never intended to share.

In the United States, 14 percent of the people control over 80 percent of the wealth. George W. Bush said on *Good Morning America* that "owning stuff is good." He wants to see all Americans enter into the "ownership society." This is the essence of the American dream and the good life. The problem with this vision is that it cannot be achieved at a time when good wage jobs are being downsized, manufacturing jobs are being outsourced, and a steadily increasing number of American families are without medical benefits. Further, once reliable pension plans have been made bankrupt by corporate leaders who pay themselves multimillion dollar salaries.

THE ABUNDANT LIFE OF JOHN 10:10

The church should be the place where the pursuit of the abundant life should be extolled. But the "prosperity gospel" is not an authentic reading of the scriptures. This book is written not only to critique those preachers who are teaching a prosperity gospel, but also to offer a prophetic critique concerning preachers who are pursuing the good life. Many are pursuing the good life rather than faithfully defining and urgently calling others to join with them in embracing a broader message of the gospel and the personal example of Jesus Christ—which had absolutely nothing to do with "the pursuit of happiness." The good life and the abundant life are not synonymous!

The idea of the "abundant life" is found within a wider passage of scripture in which Jesus seeks to differentiate his role on earth from that of other teachers who have come before him. Using the analogy of a sheepfold, Jesus says that some people enter the fold to steal or to kill the sheep; he has come to protect and provide for them. John 10:9 offers a clue into the nature of the abundant life when it says, "I am the gate; whoever enters through me will be saved, and will come in and go out and find pasture." Verse 10 then continues: "The thief comes only to steal and kill and destroy; I have come that they may have life, and have it abundantly."

It must be said that prosperity preachers who base their message on John 10:10 are in fact more reflective of the thieves and robbers who come only to steal and destroy. They drive to the sheepfold in their Bentley and Rolls Royce automobiles. They appear before the sheep dressed in the most expensive fashions and wear the costliest Rolex watches. At the end of the day, they retreat to their mansions located far away from where the sheep live. Once there, they count the money they have acquired by instructing the flock of God on how they can become wealthy and prosperous. Of course, no one prospers as much in that entire transaction as the thief who preaches that prosperity is the will of God for every believer. There is less and less prophetic preaching because more and more preachers have turned from the writings of the biblical prophets and have embraced the pursuit of profits. It is an abomination.

The theological challenge, especially so far as authentic, prophetic preaching is concerned, is to set forth the true nature of this abundant life. If the interpretation of the prosperity gospel advocates is false, then what is the truth about the abundant life mentioned by Jesus? The abundant life is a life that has been delivered from sin and death by the promise of forgiveness now, and life eternal with God. The abundant life is a life that has the assurance that God will provide for our needs so that we do not need to spend our time worrying about such things (Matthew 6:25–32). The abundant life is captured in the simple promise of Paul found in Philippians 4:19: "And my God will fully satisfy every need of yours according to his riches in glory in Christ Jesus."

If the promise is that God will supply all of our needs, then we have no need for prayer cloths that have been "anointed and prayed over" by some televangelists. If our needs are going to be fulfilled out of God's glorious riches in Christ Jesus, then why would we need to buy the video series that points us to the path of prosperity? People who live the abundant life are not obsessed about money or material things; they are simply assured that God will provide.

There is a hymn that revolves around the phrase "the Lord will make a way somehow." This assurance of God's care and provision is at the heart of the abundant life. It has little if anything to do with every passage of scripture serving as a passport to a bigger house, a larger car, or an expanding bank account. This endless desire to be financially and materially enriched is certainly what "the good life" is all about. One of the tasks of prophetic preaching, however, is to keep the secular pursuit of the good life from being confused with the spiritual position that is the abundant life. Failure to mark the distinction between those two can result in being on the wrong side of the words of Jesus in Matthew 16:26: "For what will it profit them if they gain the whole world but forfeit their life?"

PROPHETS ARE LOSING TO PROFITS

The pulpits and the pews of America are being lured into a prosperity theology where wealth and material riches can be acquired by those who learn the formula, despite overwhelming New Testament evidence to the contrary—and the formula is frequently offered by preachers who will gladly accept "donations" for their services. We hear less and less prophetic preaching because more and more preachers are focusing their messages on money and materialism. Instead of being assured of God's provision, which frees us up to serve God without worry or anxiety, the gospel is increasingly being presented in a way that suggests that the pursuit of prosperity is at the heart of the Christian life. Prosperity preaching leaves out the importance of the mission and ministry of the church and that of each individual believer. What remains is the money and the formula through which that money can come into a person's life.

IT ALL BEGAN WITH REV. IKE

It may seem to some people as if this prosperity gospel is a new phenomenon, but this approach to preaching has been building for decades outside the confines of mainline Christianity. Thirty-five years ago, this prosperity gospel had already been popularized by a New York City evangelist named Frederick Eikerenkoetter; also known as Rev. Ike. This flamboyant African American preacher headed a church he called the United Christian Evangelistic Association. From that church and by means of television he preached a message of "prosperity now."[2] People tuned in to his television show as much for entertainment as for any message they might receive.

His church building was a converted movie theatre. The stage was designed in such a way that Rev. Ike would appear on stage seated on a thronelike chair that was lifted from the lower level of the building by a motorized device. Dressed in stylish suits and wearing a red rose in his lapel, he would remind his listeners, "You can't lose with the stuff I use." His message and the medium of television set the stage for the emergence of this prosperity gospel. Of course, Rev. Ike was the outward expression of prosperity. The underlying premise and the overarching promise of his message was that others could share in his prosperity if they just followed his advice.

The popular appeal of Rev. Ike was confirmed with the release of the 1976 film, *Car Wash*, which featured Richard Pryor as Daddy Rich, a prosperity preacher who was chauffeured around Los Angeles in a gold-colored limousine with a license plate that carried the word TITHE. Most preachers saw the prosperity gospel as a gimmick that benefited the preacher far more than it did those who took the prosperity message to heart. Rev. Ike was preaching the prosperity gospel but it was not being embraced by a wide number of other preachers.

THE WORD-FAITH MOVEMENT

The emergence of an actual theological formula—introduced by Kenneth Hagin of Tulsa, Oklahoma, and known as the Word-Faith Movement—brought about a change. What has happened over the last few decades is a reading of the gospel with primary emphasis on money and wealth and on the notion that God's primary desire is to bless believers with health and wealth. This movement has been embraced by many of the most widely known national cable television preachers, including Joyce Meyer, Paula White, Juanita Bynum, Benny Hinn, Fred Price, Kenneth Copeland, and Creflo Dollar.[3] These preachers reach millions of listeners and generate hundreds of millions of dollars in annual revenue. They are a force to be reckoned with in the twenty-first century church. Theirs is a message that people are eager to hear. Theirs is also a message badly in need of a prophetic critique.

Some people refer to this Word-Faith Movement as the "name it and claim it" message.[4] It teaches that all a person needs to do is state what they want and it will be done. Of course, the only thing they are really urged to name and claim is money and prosperity. The movement invokes passages such as Matthew 7:7 and Luke 11:9–10, which say, "Ask and it will be given to you; search, and you will find; knock, and the door will be opened for you." It also makes use of what is known as "sowing a seed" with the promise that any gift sowed into a particular ministry will result in a benefit for the donor. To that end it points to passages such as Luke 6:38: "Give, and it will be given unto you. A good measure, pressed down, shaken together, running over, will be put into your lap." The key to prosperity preaching is to draw some lesson about God's desire to bless people with health and wealth out of almost every verse in the Bible. This approach to the reading of scripture can result in some extraordinary and unbelievably distorted interpretations of the meaning of a passage.

THE GOSPEL ACCORDING TO CREEFLO DOLLAR

The single most conspicuous proponent of the prosperity gospel is Creflo Dollar of the World Changers Church in Atlanta, Georgia. A *Business Week* article that examined his ministry revealed that his twenty-five-thousand-member church produces gross revenues of $70 million. Dollar himself, also known as "Cashflow Dollar," owns two Rolls Royce automobiles and flies across the country and to places around the world in his private Gulfstream-3 jet plane.[5] Creflo Dollar believes it to be the will of God for people to be prosperous. In defense of this view, he offers his understanding of Luke 4:18 and Isaiah 61:1, both of which speak about preaching good news to the poor. He says that the good news of the gospel for those who are poor is "they don't have to be poor anymore." He continues, "Jesus came to set us free from the curse of the law. Sin, death, sickness, and poverty are parts of that curse.[6]

In an attempt to make his case that scripture speaks about God's desire to make his people prosperous, Dollar offered a typical example of scriptures used in the context of a prosperity theology message broadcast on a cable television station. In 2005, he preached a Thanksgiving Day sermon from Jeremiah 30:17–19. Here is the passage in question:

> But I will restore you to health and heal your wounds,
> declares God,
> because you are called an outcast, Zion for whom
> no one cares.
> This is what God says: I will restore the fortunes of
> Jacob's tents,
> And have compassion on his dwellings; the city will be
> rebuilt on her ruins,
> And the palace will stand in its proper place.
> From them will come songs of thanksgiving and the sound
> of rejoicing.
> will add to their numbers, and they will not be decreased;
> I will bring them honor, and they will not be disdained.
> (NIV)

The preacher used the King James Version of this text which in verse 19 uses "I will multiply them" instead of the NIV phrase "add to their numbers" or the NRSV's, "I will make them many." He also opted for the KJV words "they shall not be small" for the NIV and NRSV words "they will [shall] not be disdained." His conclusion and the prosperity formula he was setting forth was the promise that if we fill our mouths with thanksgiving, God will multiply our prosperity. And even if we only have a small amount today, God is going to multiply that amount in the future.

WHEN PRAISES GO UP, BLESSINGS COME DOWN

I can remember as a child hearing people say, "When the praises go up, the blessings come down." The idea was that our financial and material prosperity was only a prayer or praise shout away. Prosperity theology assumes that it is God's will for us to be "filled," meaning that God wants all believers to be healthy and wealthy. In prosperity theology, the idea is to have God show God's "favor" upon the people. This "favor" always involves some material or financial gain. Cars, clothes, and cash are within the reach of everyone who adopts and follows the formula. All you have to do is speak your request and it will be provided. As already mentioned, prosperity preachers invoke Matthew 7:7 and Luke 11:9–10 to solidify this message.

The question that prophetic preaching must raise is whether or not asking, seeking, and knocking in search of personal prosperity is the only thing that should occupy the time and attention of Christians. Is the task of the preacher to find the silver lining of prosperity in every passage of scripture, no matter how distorted the textual analysis has to be in order to reach such a conclusion? Or is the task of prophetic preaching to warn people that preoccupation with money and material things can lead a person away from the realm of God? It was because of a preoccupation with money, leisure, and luxury that Israel began to fall out of God's favor, according to Amos that says:

> *Woe to you who are complacent in Zion,*
> *and to you who feel secure on Mount Samaria. . . .*
> *You lie on beds inlaid with ivory*
> *and lounge on your couches.*
> *You dine on choice lambs and fattened calves.*
> *You strum away on your harps like David*
> *and improvise on musical instruments.*
> *You drink wine by the bowlful and use the finest lotions,*
> *but you do not grieve over the ruin of Joseph.*
> *Therefore you will be among the first to go into exile;*
> *your feasting and lounging will end.*
> (Amos 6:1a, 4b–7 NIV)

JEREMIAH'S MESSAGE

This warning from Amos in the eighth century B.C.E. is the way to read and understand the words of Jeremiah in sixth century B.C.E. The way in which Jeremiah 30:17–19 was interpreted by Creflo Dollar may be typical of its interpretation among prosperity preachers, but it was a complete distortion of the true meaning of the text. The passage was ripped out of its sixth century B.C.E. setting, and it was disconnected from the experience of the people of Judah who had been exiled as a result of their sins.

The prosperity sermon said nothing about God restoring the nation after seventy-plus years of punishment for its having failed to uphold the covenant. There was no mention of previous sin that had to be confessed or accounted for by God's people, no word about God holding back from even further punishment or about divine mercy. Creflo's congregation and viewers were unaware that Jeremiah spoke of undeserving people being saved from God's fierce wrath over their unfaithfulness as God's covenant people.

The rich theology of Jeremiah was stripped away. The deep anguish that resided in the heart of the prophet over the plight of God's people was absent from the pronouncements of this prosperity preacher. Rather than ushering his congregation into the presence of "the weeping prophet," who decried the corruption of his society and the suffering that fell upon them by the hand of God, Creflo Dollar babbled on and on that when people fill their mouths with thanksgiving, God will multiply them—that God will bless them with wealth and well-being.

Jeremiah 30 can be considered alongside Isaiah 40 and God's promise to "comfort" the people who had been in exile but were not being allowed to return home. As Barbara Brown Taylor observed in a sermon before the Academy of Homiletics, an increasing number of preachers are "imagining a smooth road that goes around the wilderness rather than one that leads people through the wilderness with its rough places, and crooked paths and low moments." Prosperity preachers project a highway that offers exemptions from suffering, sickness, and sorrow. Isaiah preached about a highway in the wilderness that led the people of God back home after seventy-plus years of exile, an exile that was punishment for their trust in and their reliance upon such things as wealth, status, and materialism.

As the Creflo Dollar telecast continued, the content and the context of a prosperity sermon became even more apparent. No sooner had the word "multiply" been spoken by the preacher than the thousands of people who crowded the auditorium to hear the message began to shout and cheer. This was what they came to hear; the formula for receiving God's favor. "When the praises go up the blessings come down." It did not seem to matter to Creflo Dollar or his congregation that his application of the text was not remotely close to what Jeremiah 30:17–19 was about. Here was a classic case of a prophetic text being employed and directed to a pathetic application. Sadly, given the degree of biblical illiteracy that has gripped the church over the last few decades, the people who were hearing the sermon had no reason to assume that the text was being badly and brazenly misinterpreted!

LEROY THOMPSON: "I WANT MY MONEY"

Creflo Dollar is not the worst offender when it comes to the one-sided dimension of the prosperity gospel. At least Dollar made some attempt to cloak his message in the guise of a biblical text. There are other proponents of this prosperity message who are even more blatant in their replacing the "abundant life" as set forth in the New Testament with a raw pursuit of the "good life" as defined by the American pursuit of wealth and riches.

Typical of this extreme distortion of the biblical message is Leroy Thompson of the Ever Increasing Word Ministries of Darrow, Louisiana. While the membership of his local church is seventeen hundred persons (modest by prosperity theology standards), he reaches millions across the country by way of cable television, pastors' conferences, and a wide array of tapes and videos. Thompson urges his followers to recite a litany concerning the things that "belong to them." The litany states: *I want my money—God has my money—and, God, I want my money now.* The litany continues: *I am a money machine—money comes to me—I want the money that belongs to me.* Here is the "name it and claim it" message. Here is the theology that suggests that all God wants is to give us the money that is being withheld until we speak the words that will result in our receiving the blessing of wealth and prosperity.

Thompson, like most of the prosperity preachers, lives a luxurious lifestyle. Many of them do not exhibit any humility or self-sacrifice, nor do they show any evidence of having any passion for the social issues of the day in which many of their listeners are deeply embroiled. Instead, the preachers project a lifestyle of wealth and prosperity, which, they say, has come to them from God as a result of their embracing a certain way of thinking and acting. It is not uncommon for these prosperity preachers to live in mansions, drive limousines, fly in private jets, and sport the most stylish wardrobe replete with the most ornate Rolex watches being conspicuously revealed.

This conspicuous personal level of wealth serves as an incentive for those to whom they preach and to other preachers who observe the effect of their ministry. The implication is that if the people in the congregation or in the listening and viewing audience simply embrace the prosperity message being given, they too can enjoy a lavish lifestyle just like the preacher. William Martin, a sociologist from Rice University says, "The preachers' wealth is confirmation of what they are preaching."[7]

In the world of the Word-Faith Movement and in the context of the prosperity gospel, however, such displays of wealth are not to be condemned. The message is that the same prosperity can be "claimed" by anyone who adopts the formula and sows the initial seed of faith into the ministry. Of course, failure to achieve the promised prosperity points to a lack of faith on the part of the person who has received the message, not a flaw in the message or the prosperity preacher who delivered it in return for a "seed gift."

PAUL AND JAN CROUCH

One of the most reliable places to look for and listen to this Word-Faith message is on the Trinity Broadcasting Network, which can be viewed on cable television stations all over the world. The station was created and is operated by the husband and wife team of Paul and Jan Crouch. An appearance on this show is considered the top rung of the ladder for conservative, evangelical Christian television. Paul and Jan Crouch are viewed as the kingmaker or queenmaker for television preachers. Their television show is taped in a studio designed like an ornate living room, and the preaching takes place in front of a studio audience that drinks up the "cheap grace"[8] gospel regularly and generously offered. Corrupt public officials and callous public policies have nothing to fear from the people who regularly preach on this station.

PAULA AND RANDY WHITE

Recently, as part of an annual fundraising event, they invited Paula White to appear on their program. She is the popular pastor and prosperity preacher from the Without Walls International Church of Tampa, Florida. On the program, she went through her usual recitation about the importance of people "planting a seed" (give money) in order to receive "God's favor" (receive some blessing). She urged the viewers to plant a seed so that the gospel could be extended by television and satellite communications to remote places around the world. The motivation for planting the seed was simply to receive God's favor—favor defined as a personal blessing awaiting those who dialed the number on the screen.

When Paula White appears alone on her own cable television broadcast, she is equally focused on the issue of "God's favor," which is not defined as mercy or grace or love. Rather, it is defined almost exclusively as material wealth and prosperity. She then reminded people of her eight-thousand-square-foot home as a sign of what God's favor can provide those who are willing to plant a seed into her or some other ministry. She shared her ministry in Tampa, Florida, with her husband Randy White. Randy recently preached a sermon in which he was reported to have encouraged people who were broke to still find a way to give to the church. The report quoted him as saying, "If you don't have anything to give, ask the person beside you to [loan you] a hundred dollars. If they don't have it, ask them to give you a blank check."[9]

IT PAYS TO PREACH PROSPERITY

It is troublesome to note how many people crowd into churches and convention centers to hear these prosperity sermons. It is even more troublesome, however, to see how many preachers are being drawn into this practice. They see the wealth and luxurious lifestyle of these televangelists and begin to desire such a life for themselves. In a choice between sounding the alarm about human sin and human suffering or offering the promise of wealth and health, many preachers are choosing the easier and more personally rewarding road. It does not matter if the formula does not actually work for the people who are in attendance at the service; it only matters that the preacher who offers the formula for prosperity be handsomely paid for his or her efforts. The allure of prosperity preaching in both the pulpit and the pews is a major obstacle to hearing much in the way of prophetic preaching.

THE PROBLEM, NOT THE SOLUTION

The prosperity theology and the preachers who proclaim it, especially on cable television, are a major reason why prophetic preaching is so rarely heard in the American pulpit. Under the guise of John 10:10 and references to the "abundant life," more and more pulpits and pews are filled with people eager to hear how they can access the "good life." This life of abundance is much more defined by television commercials and magazine advertisements than by anything found in scripture. There is no sound, biblical basis for the claim that God's promise of personal prosperity stands at the center of the Bible or at the center of the Christian life. In twenty-first century America, prophetic preaching must make this point over and over again.

Everything in scriptures points in a direction that refutes the basic argument of prosperity theology. Matthew 6:33 is crystal clear: "Seek first [God's realm and] righteousness and all these things shall be given to you as well" (NIV). Matthew 6:19–21 is equally explicit when it says, "Do not store up for yourselves treasures on earth. . . . But store up for yourselves treasures in heaven. . . . For where your treasure is, there will your heart be also" (NIV).

The whole message of the New Testament directs against a preoccupation with material wealth. It does not speak against prosperity as much as it calls upon followers of Christ to not become preoccupied with the pursuit of such things. In Mark 10:17–25, Jesus speaks about a rich man who is unable to abandon his wealth as a precondition for following him. This story is followed by the observation, "It is easier for a camel to go through the eye of a needle than for someone who is rich to enter the kingdom of God" (v. 25). The danger is not the mere possession of wealth and prosperity; the danger is how quickly the continuing pursuit of wealth and prosperity can corrupt a person's values and relationships. This is why Paul in 1 Timothy 6:10 says, "For the love of money is the root of all kinds of evil."

PROSPERITY AMONG THE FAITHFUL IS NOT WRONG

This is not an attack upon people who, over the course of a faithful career in the ministry, manage to arrive at some degree of prosperity as a benefit of their service and stewardship. Nor is this an argument against people who earn large sums of money for the legitimate and well-received work they do every day over the course of a professional or vocational career. What is being questioned is the apparent celebration of the exorbitant and self-indulgent lifestyle that is avidly pursued by an increasing number of preachers in America, often as a result of milking and bilking their congregations through some prosperity gospel scheme.

What is also being questioned is the willingness on the part of church attendees to understand their presence at a worship service as a stepping-stone to health and wealth. Our relationship with God should not be viewed as a road map to financial success or material wealth. Rather, our relationship with God should equip us to remain faithful and focused no matter how our personal, financial, or material resources may vary from time to time.

Habakkuk 3:17–18 makes this point when it says:

> *Though the fig tree does not blossom, and no fruit is*
> *   on the vines;*
> *though the produce of the olive fails and the fields yield*
> *   no food;*

> *though the flock is cut off from the fold and there is no*
> *herd in the stalls,*
> *Yet I will rejoice in God; I will exult in the God of my*
> *salvation.*

Paul offers a similar statement in Philippians 4:11–13 when he says:

> For I have learned to be content with whatever I have. I know what it is to have little, and I know what it is to have plenty. In any and all circumstances, I have learned the secret of being well-fed and of going hungry, of having plenty and of being in need. I can do all things through him who strengthens me.

RESPONSIBILITY, NOT PROSPERITY

The problem with the prosperity gospel is not simply with what is being said. There is an equally grave problem concerning what is not being said. Prosperity for the professing Christian is the only message that is preached. The promise of wealth for those who sow the seed and follow the formula is the only promise being offered. Nothing is said about justice or injustice in the world, nor is anything said about the responsibility of Christians to care about or respond to such issues.

In the believer's pursuit of prosperity nothing is said about responding to the grinding poverty that affects tens of millions in this country and hundreds of millions around the world. Nothing is said about the two million people who occupy America's prisons and jails. Nothing is said about the thousands of U.S. military personnel who have been killed in an ill-conceived and poorly conducted war in Iraq, a nation that did not attack us on September 11, 2001, and a nation that did not have weapons of mass destruction.

As with those Justice Sunday preachers and those "patriot pastors" who limit their agenda to the issues of human sexuality and abortion, prosperity preachers limit their agenda to this single focus on the personal gain of individual believers, and to the personal enrichment of the prosperity preacher in the process. No matter how much they may attempt to say otherwise, prosperity preachers are distorting the Christian faith by their omission of what Jesus said was of greatest importance to him when he considered which persons were truly his disciples:

> I was hungry and you gave me food, I was thirsty and you gave me something to drink, I was a stranger and you welcomed me, I was naked and you gave me clothing, I was sick and you took care of me, I was in prison and you visited me. (Matt. 25:31–44)

As Warren Stewart has observed in *Interpreting God's Word in Black Preaching*, prophetic preaching "calls God's people back to their original purpose as God's elect."[10] As James Ward and Christine Ward note in *Preaching From the Prophets*, prophetic preaching "recovers the wider dimensions of the gospel, the issues of justice and righteousness, and illuminates the ways in which the community obscures them."[11] Prosperity preaching and the Word-Faith Movement have greatly obscured the wider dimensions of the gospel. It is imperative that pulpits and pews across America resonate with prophetic preaching that lifts up the wider implications of God's demand for righteousness and justice.

SEVEN

REMNANT PROPHETS
FOR A
REMNANT PEOPLE

On that day God will extend his hand
yet a second time to recover the remnant
that is left of his people.

—Isaiah 11:11

If prophetic preaching is to be restored to a vibrant place in the pulpits of America, it will be necessary for preachers to operate with a twenty-first century understanding of the message they are being called upon to declare. It is still our task to call people back from the worship of Baal and other idols, but we will need to attach twenty-first century identities to those false gods. It is still our task to demand that society care for "the least of these" among us, but we will have to attach twenty-first century names and faces and conditions to those persons. It is still our task to speak truth to power and stand against the forces of injustice as they appear not only within the broader reaches of American society, but also as they manifest themselves within the life of the contemporary church.

We need to be informed by a current job description and an updated resume for the work of prophetic preaching. It must be remembered that the themes and messages of the biblical prophets shifted and evolved over time. In the eighth century B.C.E., the message from Micah, Amos, Hosea, and the first Isaiah was a warning that a terrible judgment awaited the nation of Israel if they did not return to their covenant with God. In the seventh century, Jeremiah tried to remind the nation of Judah that what had already happened to the northern kingdom of Israel could, and would, happen to them unless they repented.

Following the fall of Jerusalem in 586 B.C.E., the message shifted again. Ezekiel tried to help the exiled people of Judah understand why they were removed from their promised land. Second Isaiah spoke about what must happen when the people were allowed to return home after their seventy-year exile in Babylon. Haggai was focused on getting the people to rebuild the Temple and resume a cultic and worship life. The content of the message by these biblical prophets was not frozen in time; the message was appropriate for the specific times in which each prophet lived and worked. What God demands from people and what prevents people from doing God's will may be quite different from one age to another.

We need an understanding of prophetic preaching that matches the times in which we live: a postmodern, nuclear-terrorist, politically polarized, grossly self-indulgent age, in which all of the world's citizens reside in a global community. We can learn from earlier generations of prophets that were faithful in and to their own generation, but we must find the will and the words to be faithful in this twenty-first century world in which we live.

TWENTY-FIRST CENTURY PROPHETIC MINISTRY

In an attempt to describe the task of prophetic preaching in the twenty-first century, I urge consideration of these words offered by Cornel West: "Prophetic beings have as their special aim to shatter deliberate ignorance and willful blindness to the suffering of others and to expose the clever forms of evasion and escape we devise in order to hide and conceal injustice." West continues by describing the work of prophetic ministry as attempting to "stir up in us the courage to care and empower us to change our lives and our historical circumstances."[1] This is an apt description for the work that awaits us: casting the light of truth on "deliberate ignorance," exposing society's blindness regarding human suffering, and equipping people with "the courage to care" and the will to take actions that will "change our lives and our historical circumstances."

This last line may be the most important and the most urgent. There are too many Christians who are only committed to a strategy that will change their lives for the better. They lack the broader interest to change the historical circumstances of poverty, oppression, marginalization, and fear that grips the lives of millions throughout this country, and the lives of billions around the world. How do you move people from being content with their own personal salvation and awaken within them an interest in and a determination to resolve the pains and problems experienced by others? Prophetic preaching stirs up the courage within people to care about and then act to change the historical circumstances that work to prevent justice and righteousness.

WHOM SHALL I SEND?

The most immediate question is who will rise to the challenge and accept the mantle of prophetic preaching? The question God raised in Isaiah 6:8 is as urgent now as it was when Isaiah heard God asking, "Whom shall I send and who will go for us?" What is needed is for men and women of faith—in all denominations, in every part of this country, and from every corner of the earth—to answer with the words of Isaiah, "Here am I. Send me." Who will walk away from the narrow agenda of Justice Sunday I and II? Who will resist the twisted theology of becoming a patriot pastor? Who will not allow the ease and enjoyment of praise and worship to obscure or crowd out the sound of prophetic preaching? Who will resist the allure of prosperity theology in order to "seek first the realm of God and God's righteousness"? God is eagerly awaiting those who are prepared to say, "Here am I. Send me!"

ONLY A REMNANT

In keeping with the motif of the biblical prophets who preached God's word at a time of false prophets and a faithless nation, it would be useful to consider the idea of the remnant. The road back to authentic prophetic preaching in America's pulpits may begin with the realization that at the turn of the twenty-first century, a remnant is all that remains in both the pulpit and the pew. Today, with so many preachers focused on matters other than prophetic preaching, there is an urgent need for preachers who will continue to pursue the agenda of justice and righteousness. This agenda was the focus of the biblical prophets and also of the prophetic preachers of the American pulpit who passed this way before.

With so many church members busy waving flags, raising holy hands, and shouting, "I want my money," there is an equally urgent need for congregations that will receive prophetic preaching. These congregations must act with courage and compassion on behalf of the people and problems that await their attention. Here again, a remnant may be all that is left, but a faithful remnant in the hands of a just and loving God can make a big difference in our world. The work of justice has always been pursued by a minority of people, a faithful few who were willing to take a stand. Large crowds and courageous action seldom come together. A million men or a million moms may march in Washington on a Saturday afternoon, but most of them are nowhere to be found when it is time to walk the streets of their own community in pursuit of justice on the local level. The recovery of prophetic preaching and prophetic action will likely begin with little more than a remnant.

What is a remnant? The remnant is an Old Testament designation that had at least three distinct meanings. The earliest concept of the remnant involved portions of the meat and grain sacrifices that were preserved for the use of the Levitical priests (Lev. 2:3, 5:13, 14:18). A second meaning of the word remnant involves people who miraculously survived a military or political crisis (Josh. 12:4, 13:12, 2 Sam, 21:2, 1 Kings 14:10). A third meaning of the word, and the one intended here, involves "the minority of Israel who would survive the calamitous purging of the wicked by God at the time of the exile and the scattering of the Jews into Babylon."[2] God will never be left without a witness; there will always be a "residue of fearless people."[3]

The catastrophes of 722 B.C.E. when the northern kingdom of Israel was conquered by Assyria and 586 B.C.E. when the southern kingdom of Judah was conquered by Babylon were the result of the majority of the covenant people breaking faith with God and turning away from their pledge to obey God's laws as commanded. These commandments were to care for the widows, orphans, and strangers in the land, and to "have no other gods before me." The destruction of the cities and the eventual destruction of the Temple of Solomon were all to be understood as God's punishment of the people of Israel for their turning away from the covenant and turning to false gods and unjust conduct.

As a sign of God's grace and mercy, however, those who had remained faithful were preserved from that destruction. This small group of people, who escaped the punishment that fell upon the majority in those nations, constituted the remnant. From the pre-exilic prophets like Amos and Micah to the prophets of the exile like Jeremiah and Ezekie, to postexilic prophets like Haggai and Zechariah, the existence of a faithful few who would be spared from destruction is a recurring theme.

This is not to suggest that God is about to send destruction upon the United States. Many people within the faith community, however, have viewed the string of events from the terrorist attacks of September 11, 2001, to the devastation of hurricanes that have recently hit this country as a sign of God's displeasure with this nation. Further, they view these events as a result of the way the church has been performing over the last twenty to thirty years. But it is being argued here that, as in the eighth and sixth centuries B.C.E., God can do great things through a remnant of faithful preachers and people who continue to heed the call for justice and righteousness and who continue to focus on the "wider implications of the message of the gospel."[4]

The remnant must stand up and speak out. It is time for the voice of prophetic preaching once again to echo across the landscape of America. It is time for the pulpits and pews of America's churches once again to consider the implications of saying, "Let justice roll down like water and righteousness like an everflowing stream." I say "reclaim" prophetic preaching in America because our nation has had the experience of hearing prophetic preaching before. There has been a remnant of prophetic preachers among us in the past who have declared "This is what God says" in the face of every moral issue and every ethical dilemma that has confronted this country over the last 250 years. There has been, at various times in our nation's history, "a residue of fearless people" who displayed courage and compassion in their pursuit of a just and equitable society. Our task in the twenty-first century is to remind ourselves of those earlier prophets and the words they spoke and the work they accomplished. Having done that, it is also our task, to the extent necessary, to keep speaking the words and keep doing the work until justice rolls down like water and righteousness like an everflowing stream.

PROPHETIC PREACHERS AND THE ANTISLAVERY MOVEMENT

Prophetic preaching was decisive in bringing slavery to an end both in this country and throughout the nineteenth-century world. The majority of people in this country had made their peace with slavery and were prepared to live with that "peculiar institution."[5] There was, however, a remnant, a residue of fearless people known as the anti-slavery movement and the Underground Railroad, who forcefully and courageously pursued a justice agenda that brought the evil system of slavery to an end. Where would this country have ended up had it not been for the courage and the compassion of Harriet Tubman, Sojourner Truth, and Frederick Douglass? Thank God for William Lloyd Garrison, Charles Sumner, Thaddeus Stevens, and the other outspoken opponents of slavery who changed the historical circumstances with which they were initially confronted.

Thank God, as well, for the prophetic preachers who made their voices heard regarding the issue of slavery. Most people are aware of the novel *Uncle Tom's Cabin* by Harriet Beecher Stowe. This 1852 novel did much to light the flames of protest against slavery in the United States. Not many people may be aware that Stowe's brother, the Rev. Henry Ward Beecher of Brooklyn, New York, was equally outspoken and courageous in this same arena. Not only was he an outspoken opponent of slavery, but in order to make a dramatic point he would actually hold mock slave auctions in his church sanctuary to bring that cruel practice closer to his congregation.[6]

One of Beecher's contemporaries, Charles G. Finney of Oberlin College, influenced by the revivalism of the Second Great Awakening, also remained vigilant in his opposition to slavery in the United States. When offered the presidency of Oberlin College in 1852, he accepted on the sole condition that the college continue to admit black students. In 1835, Oberlin had been among the first white colleges to admit black students. Equally important, Finney allowed Oberlin College to become a stop on the Underground Railroad that aided runaway slaves in their escape from southern slavery to northern freedom and on into Canada.[7] Finney did not simply talk against slavery; he took concrete steps to help slaves escape and then to become educated. Preachers today need to reclaim the prophetic fervor and the personal courage of Beecher and Finney.

Most students of preaching are familiar with the name Joseph Parker, the British preacher of the mid-nineteenth century who filled the City Temple in London with some of the greatest preaching ever heard. Another preacher of the same era, Theodore Parker (no relation), was undoubtedly the most relentless antislavery preacher in the United States. This biblically based, prophetically inspired preacher refused to be silent about an issue he believed to be a moral outrage and a national scandal.[8] The names of black preachers like Morris Brown, Henry Highland Garnet, Henry McNeil Turner, and Daniel Payne should be added to any list of prophetic preachers who stood up and spoke out against the evil of slavery in the nineteenth century.

THE LINGERING PROBLEM OF RACISM

In 1866, slavery officially ended with the adoption of the Thirteenth Amendment to the U.S. Constitution. This event, however, fell far short of bringing in an era of justice and righteousness. Slavery was followed by rigid laws of racial segregation, the Jim Crow doctrine of "separate but equal," sharecropping that virtually enslaved three additional generations of African Americans on land they worked but did not own, and one hundred years of terrorism led by the Ku Klux Klan. Their racist tactics outmatched anything the Department of Homeland Security could imagine in terms of ferocity and intimidation. Thus, while slavery has ended, the work of justice within the arena of racial diversity and the equality of all persons must continue.

Preachers should be careful not to do this work based solely upon the founding documents of our nation, although the wording and intent in the Declaration of Independence, regarding all people being created equal, is good to mention. Prophetic preaching cannot be based entirely on secondary sources. It must be rooted and grounded in the primary text of the scriptures themselves. We need to see God sending Jonah to preach in the Assyrian capitol of Nineveh because even though the prophet Jonah did not like "those people," the people of that Gentile city were dear to the heart of God. We need to see Jesus being threatened with death in Luke 4 because he dared to suggest to a Jewish audience that the God of Israel could possibly love a Phoenician widow or a Syrian general as much as he loved them. We need to hear Jesus vetoing the acceptable prejudice of the first century of the common era by giving value to a man he called "a good Samaritan."

Over and over again, the Bible calls us away from the assumptions of racial prejudice or racial preferences. Nowhere is this more clearly stated than in Acts 17:26a: "From one ancestor he made all nations to inhabit the whole earth. . . ." That same motif of all nations being the handiwork of God and being the object of God's desired work of redemption and salvation is made manifest in the composition of the crowd that heard Peter's sermon on the first Pentecost in Acts 2. A consideration of the nations present in that crowd would reveal people from Europe, Asia, Africa, and the Mediterranean region, all of whom were joined together into the body of Christ. Homogeneity, which is such an important principle for American church life, was not at all important for the early church.

APARTHEID: WRONG BECAUSE UNGODLY

Those who preach the gospel of Jesus Christ in the United States would do well to consider the courage and compassion displayed by Desmond Tutu, Alan Boesak, and other less notable preachers who took a moral stand against apartheid in South Africa. While Nelson Mandela was imprisoned on Robbin Island as a result of his actions against that brutal system of racism, those preachers were boldly speaking out against the practice of apartheid and the whites-only, minority government. In his book *God Has a Dream,* Tutu says, "To oppose injustice and oppression is not something that is merely political. No, it is profoundly religious."[9] He continues, "God demands the obedience of our whole person in opposing injustice. For not to oppose injustice is to disobey God."[10]

Here is the point: prophetic preaching cannot and must not be anchored in the words of Thomas Jefferson. This is especially true since as a slaveholder Jefferson did not practice what he wrote concerning all men being created equal. No, our prophetic preaching and the actions they spawn must be rooted in the language of scripture and the words of God. The scriptures must provide the content for our prophetic preaching, and as a side benefit they also must provide an unassailable authority that can be found in no other text.

CIVIL RIGHTS: A PROPHETIC MOMENT

When the Southern Christian Leadership Conference organized in 1957, it did so with a clear mission statement;

"to redeem the soul of America."[11] The people who gathered in Atlanta for that founding event were essentially a group of preachers who were possessed by a prophetic zeal for justice and righteousness. Their focus was not simply on the Fourteenth Amendment and "equal protection under the law." Their focus was on the Exodus story and on God sending Moses to Pharaoh with the words, "Let my people go." Out of the tradition of biblical prophets, God blessed our nation with the presence of preachers ranging from Martin Luther King Jr. to James Lawson, Ralph Abernathy, Wyatt Tee Walker, C. T. Vivian, Andrew Young, Fred Shuttlesworth, Walter Fauntroy, Jesse Jackson, James Bevel, Kelly Miller Smith, Thomas Kilgore, CK. Steele, and many more. They continued the work of the abolitionists into the twentieth century.

As Mark Lewis Taylor reminds us in his book *Religion, Politics, and the Christian Right,* "being prophetic, 'speaking before' others, especially speaking to the powerful, who damage and oppress the public life we seek to build together, is a function that can be shared by many outside and inside the religious traditions."[12] That would suggest that the American civil rights movement was driven not only by ordained clergypersons preaching prophetically from pulpits. This movement was equally defined by nonclergy acting out of the values of the biblical prophets. These modern day prophets stood up and spoke out for justice in Birmingham, Selma, and Montgomery, Alabama; on Freedom Rides or protest marches; or during sit-ins at a lunch counter. Taylor's broadening of who can act and speak prophetically makes room for John Lewis, James Farmer, Medgar Evers, Charles Sherrod, Bob Moses, Roy Wilkins, and Stokely Carmichael to be viewed as prophetic figures.

The movement was also never a male-only domain—although some who recount and report that history might leave that impression. Taylor opens the door for

Fannie Lou Hamer, who worked for voting rights for African Americans in Mississippi, or Daisy Bates, who organized and undergirded the nine students that integrated Central High School in Little Rock, Arkansas, to be seen as prophetic figures. The same can be said about Septima Clark, whose citizenship classes trained people to register voters. She also headed the NAACP in South Carolina even after the group was outlawed in that state. This decision resulted in her being fired from her job as a public school teacher.

The list of prophetic women in the civil rights movement would also include Diane Nash Bevel, who was a leading member of the Student Nonviolent Coordinating Committee (SNCC); Ella Baker, who had been instrumental in the organization of SNCC and was also the first executive director of the Southern Christian Leadership Conference (SCLC); Vivian Malone and Autherine Lucy, who in 1964 on separate occasions integrated the University of Alabama; and Charlene Hunter Gault, who integrated the University of Georgia in 1962. Before any of these women was Constance Baker Motley, who with Thurgood Marshall served on the legal team that won the 1954 landmark ruling known as Brown versus Board of Education. Finally, there was the mother of the movement, Rosa Parks, whose courageous decision in 1955 to refuse any further compliance with segregation in public transportation launched the bus boycott in Montgomery, Alabama, that brought Martin Luther King Jr. to the forefront of national leadership.

Each of these persons, men and women, lay and clergy, remind us of the legacy of prophetic speech and action that should "stir up in us the courage to care and empower us to change our lives and our historical circumstances."[13] If prophetic preaching is to be renewed and restored in our society in the twenty-first century, we will need to hear from men and women, from laity and clergy, and from people of all ethnic backgrounds and denominational groupings who are willing to speak the words and do the work of justice.

PROPHETIC PREACHERS AND WOMEN'S RIGHTS

One of the stories that need to be told and retold involves those women preachers who modeled prophetic ministry in the face of rejection and resistance as they declared their call to ministry. These prophetic women challenged the church to open its doors to the ministry gifts of all of God's children. In 1809, even before the formal organization of the African Methodist Episcopal Church (AME), the prophetic voice of Jarena Lee was heard as she urged Richard Allen to ordain her as an elder in that church. She refused to "stay in her place," reminding people in her autobiography, "Why should it be thought impossible, heterodox, or improper for a woman to preach, seeing the Savior died for the woman as well as the man?"[14] In 1894, it was Jarena Lee (and later Julia Foote) who was the first woman to be ordained as an elder in the African Methodist Episcopal Zion church. Her courage and convictions planted seeds that eventually sprouted in the form of the election and consecration of another woman, Vashti Murphy McKenzie, as the first female bishop of the AME church in 2000.[15]

Nannie Helen Burroughs was a prophet among us when she challenged the National Baptist Convention to make room for the talents and gifts of women. Moreover, she displayed both courage and compassion when she used her position within the Women's Department of that convention to reach out to white women in America. She challenged them to use their influence within the white communities of this country to bring an end to every form of racism and discrimination, most notably the Jim Crow separate but equal laws in public transportation.[16] Burroughs came under federal surveillance when she spoke truth to power and condemned President Woodrow Wilson for his refusal to support any form of antilynching legislation.[17]

Betty Zink-Sawyer, in her book *From Preachers to Suffragists*, reminds us of three women—Antoinette Brown Blackwell, Olympia Brown, and Anna Howard Shaw. These women combined the work of suffragette with the call to ministry and challenged American society on both counts: a woman's right to vote and a woman's right to preach the gospel.[18] Blackwell was the first woman to be ordained by any denomination in the United States when she was ordained by the Congregational Church in 1853.[19] Zink-Sawyer reminds the reader that the woman's rights movement emerged out of the abolitionist movement. She states, "If the antislavery movement provided women reformers with an incipient opportunity to engage in public rhetoric as they promoted a cause, the woman's rights movement provided an opportunity for the blossoming of their rhetorical skills as they claimed public space to promote their own equality."[20]

None of these women, black or white, represented the majority opinion at that time. They were voices crying in the wilderness. Zink-Sawyer reminds us, "The public silence of women was among the infallible matters most nineteenth-century Americans believed to be decreed by the Bible."[21] Instead of conforming to that assumption, these women were a prophetic remnant, "a residue of fearless people" who boldly made their appeal for justice and righteousness within the broader society. Preachers today do not have to imagine what prophetic preaching sounds like, nor do they have to wonder about the kinds of issues that can and should be made subject to a prophetic critique. All we have to do is look back to those nineteenth-century prophets whose voices and values helped to reshape the nation.

WOMANIST AND FEMINIST THEOLOGIANS

The role of women in society in general and in the church in particular is far from a settled question so far as many Christians are concerned. The most prophetic voices among us today may well be the voices of women who continue to push both church and society beyond the single issue of race. They do so to confront and resolve the equally troubling issues of gender (feminists) and gender and poverty or class (womanists). Theologians such as Jacqueline Grant, ethicists such as Emily Townes and Katie Cannon, biblical scholars such as Clarice Martin and Renita Weems, as well as preachers such as Suzan Johnson Cook, Teresa Fry Brown, and Carolyn Knight, who operate out of these perspectives, must be encouraged in their work and "heard" (*shema,* or heeded in Hebrew) when they offer their prophetic critique.

Feminist and womanist preachers are, in the language of Rebecca Chopp, doing "saving work." Building upon that phrase, Joy Ann McDougall writes, "Doing saving work signified something more than redressing gender injustices or adding women's stories to the church's story. It pointed to the distinctive practices that women are undertaking, practices that offered a fresh reading of Christianity.[22] Chopp continues to point out the benefits and possibilities of feminist voices when she says:

> Many women theologians are using insights and practices from feminist theology in order to address broader social and ethical questions confronting the church. These feminists projects aim at something more than creating a women's-only discourse. They signal a mainstreaming of feminist discourse so that it might transform the practice of Christian communities and contribute to the flourishing of all of God's creation."[23]

In the face of these insightful contributions to the present and future life of the church, it is painful to hear male pastors still debating whether or not to recognize the ministry gifts of women. As a pastor, it is disheartening to hire female associates in my local church as a step toward preparing them for a position as senior pastor only to discover that few black Baptist churches across the country are willing to consider them for that position. As a seminary professor of preaching who listens to men and women when they preach in class, it is tragic to consider the wonderful gifts and the unique insights lost to those churches that refuse to embrace the concept of women in ministry.

TEXTS OF TERROR

Paul's writings in 1 Corinthians 14:34–35 and 1 Timothy 2:9–15 have become texts of terror. According to Phyllis Trible, they are used because they lock women into a first-century social location, accomplished through a precritical method of textual analysis. Those who are still resisting the role of women in ministry are living in a biblical and theological time warp. In all other ways, the world and the church have changed—but not regarding women in ministry. It is the past practice of Second Temple Israel that defines our present and our future practice in this area.

The role of women in ancient Israel is not the role of women in twenty-first century America. Much prophetic preaching is needed on this point. Did Paul really mean to suggest that women, who today serve as governors, mayors, legislators, judges, physicians, lawyers, astronauts, teachers, scholars, corporate executives, and media moguls, cannot be entrusted with the preaching of the gospel? Demetrius Williams of Tulane University is correct when he observes in his book *An End to This Strife*, "There are no hermeneutical or exegetical grounds to use 1 Corinthians 14:33b–36 (or any passage of scripture for that matter) to justify the silencing and elimination of women's voices and participation in the worship service or as ordained preachers and pastors."[24]

If the role of women in society must remain unchanged from the days of the early church, then any opposition to slavery should also have been resisted, since Paul also seemed to accept the reality of that evil institution in Romans 13:1–7. The same conclusion could be reached by reading 1 Peter 2:13–20. I do not know a single preacher, black or white, who, in opposing women in ministry on the grounds of biblical teaching, would be willing to return to the yoke of slavery because it too was a biblically acceptable practice. Demetrius Williams further observes, "African American churches can no longer advocate racial equality on biblical grounds and at the same time support sexism in the churches using the same Bible.[25]

You would think that Galatians 3:28 would have settled this question long ago: "there is neither Jew or Greek, there is no longer slave or free, there is no longer male and female; for all of you are one in Christ Jesus." You would also think that some attention by those who resist the idea of women in ministry would be given to 1 Corinthians 11:5. Here Paul speaks about women who pray or prophesy covering their heads, right alongside of a comment about who should keep their heads uncovered when they pray and prophesy. The issue here is not silence; the issue is form and formality.

There is plenty of prophetic work that needs to be done in this area. Returning to the opening definition of prophetic ministry by Cornel West, there are many areas of "deliberate ignorance and willful blindness as well as many clever forms of evasion" that need to be addressed by people of courage and compassion.

ANTIWAR ACTIVISM

Some of the most courageous voices to be heard in the last fifty to sixty years have been those preachers who have been willing to stand up and speak out against the inhumanity and wastefulness of war. No less a figure in the history of the American pulpit is Harry Emerson Fosdick, former senior pastor of Riverside Church in New York City, who led the way in this area. His 1933 sermon, "To the Unknown Soldier," was an apology for his own defense of war during World War I and an apology to all the men he had counseled to serve in that conflict dubbed "the war to end all wars."[26]

Riverside Church was the site from which many other prophetic preachers took their stand against war. On April 4, 1967, Martin Luther King Jr. preached his famous sermon "A Time to Break Silence," in which he came out against the costly and ultimately unconscionable war in Vietnam. A decade after that, William Sloane Coffin became senior pastor of Riverside Church. From this position of power, he not only opposed all forms of conventional warfare, but he also led the way in pointing out the dangers of warfare in the nuclear age through his involvement with an organization known as SANE/FREEZE.

These men were not alone in their prophetic warnings about the dangers and wastefulness of war. The brothers and Roman Catholic priests Daniel and Philip Berrigan opposed the Vietnam War with their bodies as well as their words. Rabbi Abraham Joshua Heschel was a leader in the antiwar group known as Clergy and Laity Concerned about Vietnam. Of course there was the ideological equivalent of "patriot pastors" in the 1960s and 1970s that were busy waving flags and slapping bumper stickers on their cars urging others to "support our troops." Where were they when more than fifty-eight thousand of those troops came home in body bags? More importantly, where were they when the United States withdrew its troops from Vietnam, leaving that country as the communist society that it continues to be to this day?

Opposition to war was never as simple as rejecting aggression or embracing pacifism or nonviolence. What made their opposition to war a matter of prophetic ministry was their ability to see the connection between any act of war and the devastation that war brings upon society as a whole. What ties together the Vietnam War and the conflict in Iraq are the human and social costs attached. King understood that the United States could not invest what had been promised to fight a War on Poverty when the nation was spending five hundred thousand dollars daily on the war in Vietnam. He also understood the cruel irony involved in asking soldiers from America's inner cities to fight a war for freedom in Southeast Asia when many basic freedoms were being denied to them in their own hometowns.

In 2006, at a time when our own nation is in desperate need of resources to rebuild our aging cities and our crumbling infrastructure, the pulpits of America must reverberate with the words, "This is what God says." At a time when we need to provide quality education and quality medical care for all of our citizens, our government has already pumped $400 billion into a war in Iraq. As an additional $150 billion has been requested and/or approved, the time is ripe for the voice of the prophet who will cry aloud and spare not (Isa. 58:1). In an article in *The Living Pulpit*, I continue this line of thought by saying:

> The nation announces a war on HIV/AIDS but does not fund the initiative or disburse the funds that have been allocated. The nation talks about an educational program called "No Child Left Behind." But does not fund any programs to make that happen. . . . We deploy an inadequate number of troops to actually preserve the peace in Iraq, and just as important and for the same reason of costs, we do not deploy enough personnel

to protect our own borders against either illegal immigration or illegal drugs."[27]

While America seems to have an endless supply of money to direct wars in Afghanistan and Iraq, we cannot properly fund our public schools. We cannot provide medical insurance or quality care for all of our citizens. Our nation's bridges, tunnels, highways, and electric grids need massive overhauls. The great city of New Orleans, once attacked by the fury of Hurricane Katrina and the failure of its levee system, has been attacked a second time by a federal government that is more interested in rebuilding Baghdad than it is in rebuilding its own Gulf Coast communities.

William Sloane Coffin reminds us of the hospitals, schools, libraries, houses, and infrastructure that could be purchased by half of the two trillion dollars spent on defense during the Reagan administration alone. He also points out "the army of ten thousand nurses and ten thousand teachers that could be supported by that same defense spending between 1980 and 1988; with tens of billions of dollars left over.[28] The cost to destroy Iraq and to constantly prepare for wars around the world is the gradual decline of the quality of life and the commitment to the neediest within our own society.

The war in Iraq in particular, and all war when considered together, comes with a very high cost in human life. The United States led a coalition of other nations in invading Iraq and launching a war on terror even though Iraq had no involvement in the tragic events of September 11, 2001. We were assured that "Saddam Hussein has weapons of mass destruction." After the deaths of nearly three thousand U.S. military personnel and untold numbers of Iraqis, no such weapons or the capability to make them were ever found. Soon there will be more U.S. fatalities in the Iraqi war than there were fatalities on September 11, 2001. What will have been accomplished by this reckless venture?

It was Osama Bin Laden and his Al Qaeda organization who took credit, not only for the September 11 attacks, but also for earlier attacks on the World Trade Center, the USS Cole while docked in Yemen, and on U.S. embassies in Kenya and Tanzania. The White House announced that Bin Laden was "wanted, dead or alive." Today, most of Afghanistan is controlled by warlords; most of Iraq is threatened by insurgents with roadside bombs and suicide vests; and Osama Bin Laden remains at large.

It is an important milestone that Iraq held elections for a national legislature in December 2005, but how long and at what cost of human and economic resources will democracy in Iraq be undergirded by the U.S. military? More importantly, who really believes that a democratically elected government in Iraq will bring an end to terrorism or to the expressed grievances that fuel suicide bombers and their sponsors?

The irony and hypocrisy of this current war is revealed by the U.S. government's support of Osama Bin Laden when he fought with the Mujahadin in Afghanistan against the occupation of that country by the Soviet Union. The U.S. government also openly supported Saddam Hussein when he led a war against the neighboring country of Iran. Today, two of our former allies have become our enemies in the "global war on terror," and our government seems blind to the reality that dropping five-hundred-pound bombs in places where civilian deaths are all but certain is itself an act of terror.

We condemn the treatment of prisoners held by the insurgents in Iraq. Yet, at the same time, U.S. Secretary of State Condoleeza Rice offers a torturous statement about our treatment of prisoners held without charge in Abu Ghraib prison in Iraq or at the Guantanamo Bay naval base where more uncharged and untried "enemy combatants" are being held over the protests of nations around the world. Our moral authority as a nation is eaten away with every charge of prisoner abuse as well as with every veiled attempt to justify such actions on the basis of September 11, 2001, and the war on terror. We should be informed by a line from the hymn "God of Grace and God of Glory" written by Harry Emerson Fosdick that warns, "Save us from weak resignation to the evils we deplore."[29] We cannot win the war on terror by becoming like the people whose actions we seek to condemn.

Our preemptive U.S. war effort has little to do with the rights of a nation for self-defense. It has much more to do with our national interests in oil reserves and reconstruction contracts for Halliburton Corporation, a corporation once headed by Vice President Dick Cheney. Halliburton has been accused of overbilling the U.S. government by hundreds of million dollars for everything from food to supplies. Now is no time for blind acts of patriotism that overlook or underestimate the skyrocketing social, economic, and human costs of this war. Prophetic preaching is needed in this area. And while it may prove to be unpopular among some within our society, it is consistent with the work of the biblical prophets, and it is also consistent with our own nineteenth- and twentieth-century predecessors. Their preaching stirred up themselves and others to be courageous in changing their own lives and also initiating great changes within their historical circumstances.[30]

THE VOICE OF THE PROPHET MUST BE HEARD AGAIN

In every generation, the business of prophetic preaching is to confront the great moral and ethical issues that confound the world from the perspective of the moral authority of scripture. The church cannot be allowed to lose sight of "the wider dimensions of the gospel."[31] The church cannot be allowed to sit on the sidelines of history squabbling over abortion and human sexuality, waving flags as patriot pastors, lifting up holy hands without extending helping hands, or pursuing formulas for wealth and prosperity while poverty, starvation, violence, bigotry, and greed go unchecked and unchallenged.

God needs us to get busy speaking the words and doing the work of justice and righteousness. The church and the world are desperately in need of the renewal of prophetic preaching. The question is the same today as it was in Isaiah 6:8: "Who shall we send, and who will go for us?" In this present age, we need preachers and nonclergy prophetic Christians to answer the call as did Isaiah and say: "Here am I. Send me!"

A BENEDICTION

As the call for prophetic preaching is answered in pulpits across this country, and God willing around the world, it should never be assumed that we are entering this task alone or with only our own available resources. The best way to end all that has been set forth in these pages is to use a text closely associated with Advent.

> *Every warrior's boot used in battle*
> *and every garment rolled in blood*
> *will be destined for burning,*
> *will be fuel for the fire.*
> *For to us a child is born,*
> *to us a son is given,*
> *and the government will be on his shoulders.*
> *And he will be called*
> *Wonderful Counselor, Mighty God,*
> *Everlasting Father, Prince of Peace.*
> *Of the increase of his government and peace*
> *there will be no end.*
> *He will reign on David's throne*

and over his kingdom,
establishing and upholding it
with justice and righteousness
from that time on and forever.
The zeal of God Almighty
will accomplish this. (Isa. 9:5–7 NIV)

Maranatha. *Come, Sovereign Jesus* (Rev. 22:20).

Under God
Is a Good Place
to Be

This sermon is included as an example of the kind of preaching this book has been trying to explain. It is a combination of contemporary issues in society as viewed through the lens of faith and then shared in the context of a Sunday morning worship service. I preached it on November 14, 2005, at Olivet Institutional Baptist Church of Cleveland, Ohio, where Dr. Otis Moss Jr. is the pastor. The text for the sermon is from Psalm 139:1–14 and Ephesians 3:20–21.

O ver the last few years, several court actions and/or judicial rulings have been offered regarding the constitutionality of reciting the Pledge of Allegiance to the American flag, all because the pledge includes the phrase "one nation under God. . . ."

Those who raise this as a concern do so out of their defense of the idea of "separation of church and state," a phrase that, by the way, does not appear anywhere in the

U.S. Constitution. That phrase was written by Thomas Jefferson to the Danbury Baptist Association of Connecticut in 1802. Some raise it out of their position of atheism, and they object to their children having to speak these words, "under God."

Whatever the concerns of others might be, let me begin by saying that of all the words in the Pledge of Allegiance, the words "under God" cause me the least concern. If I were going to tinker with the language of the Pledge of Allegiance, I would not start with the words "under God." I might start with the words "one nation." Are we really one nation when so few people control so much of the wealth and power? Are we really one nation when so many people are homeless, living without medical insurance, trapped in minimum wage jobs, and losing their jobs in record numbers while corporate executives plunder their companies and then retire with unbelievable wealth?

Look at Enron, WorldCom, Adelphia, Martha Stewart, and the other corporate giants who got rich through shady stock deals while the workers in those companies lost their jobs and the stockholders lost their life savings. I am not troubled by being "under God." What worries me is the pretense we continue to make about being "one nation."

When African Americans can constitute 13 percent of the nation's general population, but more than 70 percent of the nation's prison population, I wonder about the phrase "liberty and justice for all." When over two million people in the United States are confined in prisons or living under the jurisdiction of the criminal justice system, and most of them are nonviolent drug offenders who would do much better under treatment than under incarceration, I wonder about liberty and justice for all.

When I can sit on the Grand Jury for four months and never see a single black assistant county prosecutor come into the room, I wonder about the words "liberty and justice for all." When not a single African American male sits as a judge on any common pleas or appeals court anywhere in the state of Ohio, and when the only black member of the U.S. Supreme Court is Clarence Thomas, I really wonder about the words "with liberty and justice for all."

I could go on and ask about that word "republic." That word means that we are supposed to be a nation where no one is more important than anyone else and where everybody's vote is supposed to count. What kind of republic allows what happened in Florida during the 2000 election? Al Gore won the popular vote, meaning more Americans voted for Gore than voted for George Bush. Yet, because of something called the electoral college, George Bush won the election.

In order for that to happen, it has been alleged that people were turned away from the voting booths in Florida. Thousands of names were unfairly removed from the voting rolls. Thousands of votes that would likely have gone to Al Gore were deemed to be invalid and were not counted. Even after all of that, the election was too close to call, and so the U.S. Supreme Court—not the majority of the voters in the United States of America—"selected" the president. I am not nearly as bothered by the words "under God" as I am by the word "republic."

Then comes the word "indivisible." This word carries the sense of our being so closely united that nothing could create any division within our body politic. Whatever else, in America, we are hardly indivisible. We are divided by race: black and white, Hispanic and Asian, Native American and illegal immigrants. We are divided by region: inner cities and outer ring suburbs, "blue" states and "red" states, rust-belt cities and sun-belt regions. Someone should ask the people of New Orleans and other Gulf Coast communities if the nation's response to the catastrophic events of Hurricane Katrina and Hurricane Rita suggest to them that our nation is indivisible.

In my opinion, the words "under God" are the most important words in the Pledge of Allegiance. I say that for three reasons, the first of which is simply that in a world that was created by God's power and is sustained by God's grace we are all physically under God. That is the message of Psalm 139: there is no place on earth or in the heavens above that is not under God. This is as simple as the doctrine of sovereignty. As big and expansive as this country is, it is only part of God's earth, and the earth is only one of God's planets in this solar system, and this solar system is only one of the clusters of stars in the vast reaches of God's heavens.

Genesis 1:1 says, "In the beginning . . . God created the heavens and the earth." God is not a concept to be agreed upon or rejected by the feeble minds of men and women. God is the maker of heaven and earth. God holds the whole world in God's hand. We are physically located under God. "The earth is God's and all that is in it, the world, and those that live in it" (Psa. 24:1).

There is a philosophical and a lyrical way to make this first point. The philosophical answer comes from Thomas Anselm (1033–1109), who in his ontological argument for God's existence held that "God is that than which nothing greater can even be conceived." The lyrical answer comes from traditional Negro spiritual that says, "My Lord is so high you can't get over him, so wide you can't get around him, so deep you can't get under him. You must come in, by, and through the door." As a Christian who is informed by the reading of scripture, I accept the fact that I am under God.

I am amazed when I consider how people like us, who are prone to pain and sickness, and who eventually yield to disease and to death, take it upon ourselves to decide whether or not we want to be under God. When I watch the seasons rotate and hear the sparrows sing, I know and rejoice that I am under God. When flowers burst into colors that no artist can fully match and that no camera can completely capture, I know and I rejoice that I am under God. When my own body is sick, when my own path is cluttered with troubles and sorrows, do not talk to me about what is and is not constitutionally acceptable language. In that hour, know that my whole life stands at peace under God, and my soul will cry out, "Father, I stretch my hands to thee, no other help I know. If thou withdraw thyself from me, whither shall I go?"[1] It is one thing to debate this business in a court-room or a classroom, but when you enter into a sick-room or a dying room, don't you want this world to be under God?

There is a second way in which I choose to under-stand the phrase, "under God." The psalmist says it is God who searches us and knows us and holds us ac-countable for our thoughts and our deeds. Our ultimate accountability is to God. I may pledge my allegiance to the flag of the United States of America as a matter of po-litical affiliation, but my conscience and my conduct must always be considered as I seek to live "under God." My sense of justice and fairness are not shaped by America, whether that means Wall Street or Hollywood or Madison Avenue. My values and my moral convictions must always remain "under God." In both physical posi-tion and private conscience, I am far more subordinate to God than to anybody or anything on earth.

This independence of conscience and the willingness to conduct one's life in accordance with that conscience is what allowed people throughout the years to resist the evils done by their governments. Moses could stand against Pharaoh, Nathan the prophet could stand against King David, John the Baptist could stand against Herod Antipas, and Jesus could stand against Pilate because all of them were under God. Most of the great crusades for a just and fair society were led by people who opposed a corrupt government as a result of having a conscience that was under God.

The German pastor and philosopher Dietrich Bonhoeffer was killed by the Nazis in Flossenburg concentration camp on April 9, 1945. That was just a few days before the camp was liberated by the Allies at the end of World War II. This man was living in the United States when Hitler began his ruthless rise to power, and all of his friends urged him to remain safely in this country. But Bonhoeffer believed that he had no right to live in peace and safety while people in his homeland were living in terror. He returned to Germany and helped lead the opposition to the Nazis. One of the men who worked with him and who also died at the hands of the Nazis was his brother-in-law, Hans von Dohnanyi, the father of Christoph von Dohnanyi, who just retired as musical director of the Cleveland Orchestra. These men and many others took the stand they did because while their bodies were in Germany, their consciences and sense of human decency were "under God."

In this country, slavery was the most evil thing men ever established. Millions of people were forced from their homes in Africa, transported for two months across the Atlantic Ocean, sold into lifelong bondage, and worked like animals until they died. Make no mistake about it, it took more than Abraham Lincoln and the Emancipation Proclamation to end slavery. Slavery was brought to an end by people like John Brown, Sojourner Truth, Frederick Douglass, Harriet Tubman, and other nameless men and women who lived in this country but whose minds and hearts were under God.

The government alone did not end segregation and Jim Crow laws in the 1964 Civil Rights Bill. They were ended by Rosa Parks and Martin Luther King Jr., by Daisy Bates and Fred Shuttlesworth, by Septima Clark and James Meredith, by John Lewis and Autherine Lucy.

Justice came as a result of thousands of other men, women, and children whose bodies may have been in America, but whose conscience and spirit and faith were clearly under God. The right to vote for millions of African Americans throughout the South was not attained by the 1965 Voting Rights Act. That right, which had long been denied by people who pledged their allegiance to the flag, was brought about by the courage and sacrifice of the people who marched from Selma to Montgomery, Alabama. Many of them lost their lives on that dangerous and difficult march, but they pressed on because while their bodies were in Alabama their souls and spirits were "under God." I have no problem with being "under God," because that is what allows me to stand up and speak out when people in government practice injustice. So I say again, being "under God" is a good place to be.

Let me mention the third reason why I don't mind being "under God," and let me link it to the passage in Ephesians 3:20–21. I don't mind being under the God who "is able to accomplish abundantly far more than all we can ask or imagine." The apostle Paul clearly establishes the difference between God and any government on earth. God is able to do. Think of all the things the United States government is not able to do. We were told that bringing Osama Bin Laden to justice was the top priority for our country, but the CIA and the FBI are not able to do it. They cannot find him, much less to bring him to justice. Thirty years ago, this country declared a war on drugs, but thirty years later drug use and crimes related to drug use are at an all-time high. Our government is not able to do it.

How is it possible that we can put a man on the moon and send satellites into space, but we cannot build a car that lasts for at least ten years and can get fifty miles per gallon of gas? There are some things we cannot do and there are some other things that we will not do. The good thing about God is that God is able to do. If we put our whole faith in God and devoted our lives to God's control, God would show us how to bring peace on earth, even to the troubled region of the Middle East. God is able to do it. If we put our faith in God and committed ourselves to live by God's teachings we could end hunger and poverty throughout the world. Governments cannot or will not do it, but God is able to do it.

God, our heavenly father, is able to do what my own earthly father was unable or unwilling to do. My father abandoned our family when I was ten years old. He took half of the household furniture and most of the money and left my mother, my brother, and me to fend for ourselves. I learned a lot about the "love of the church" when my family was abandoned. The women in our local church pulled away from my mother rather than surrounding her in support because they thought that she, as a single woman, might become interested in or interesting to their husbands.

My mother tried to enroll in the music department at Moody Bible Institute in Chicago. She was the church organist, and she wanted to increase and perfect her skills. She was denied admission to that "Bible" institute, however, because she was a divorcee. It did not matter to them that she had been abandoned by her husband. There was no room at Moody Bible Institute for an abandoned, divorced church musician.

What people were unable or unwilling to do, however, was more than offset by what God was able to do. God took us and sustained us and made a way out of no way for us until we had come through that storm in life. I remember a high school guidance counselor telling me that as a poor child from a broken home who did not have a mind for college-level work, I should not aspire to a college education. I should just seek a career as a carpenter or an auto mechanic.

I came home and told my mother that I could not go to college because the guidance counselor told me that we were poor, that our home was broken, and that I did not have a mind for college-level work. My mother assured me that only three people had a vote or a voice on my future: God, her, and me. She told me that she was voting for me to go to college. She told me to vote the same way. Then she assured me that God had already voted in the affirmative and would provide the means as well.

I will never forget the day I walked across the stage to receive my Doctor of Ministry degree from Princeton Theological Seminary. My mother met me at the bottom of the stairs and asked me, "Where is the guidance counselor who told us that we did not have a mind for college-level work?" No, "God is able to accomplish abundantly far more than all we can ask or imagine."

This doxology by Paul is amazing, because it sounds as if Paul cannot say enough about the power of God, so he continues to compound his praise. First he says, "God is able . . ." Then he says, "God is able to accomplish . . ." Then he adds to that by saying, "God is able to accomplish abundantly . . ." That does not seem to be enough for Paul, so he goes on to say, "God is able to accomplish abundantly far more . . ." That might have been enough for most people, but not for Paul, and so he then says, "God is able to accomplish abundantly far more than all we can ask . . ." Having said that, Paul makes this final claim when he declares, "God is able to accomplish abundantly far more than all we can ask or imagine."

The one thing that most limits the power of God at work in our lives is our own imagination. We have not yet fully comprehended how great God truly is, and how much God can actually do. If God could give life to Abraham and Sarah when both of them were old and when Sarah had been barren all of her life, then God can do more than anything we can ask or think. If God could split the Red Sea for Moses; bring down the walls of Jericho for Joshua; defeat the Midianites for Gideon; bring down Goliath for little David; lock the lions' jaws for Daniel; and raise Jesus, Lazarus, and the daughter of Jairus from the dead, then God is able to accomplish abundantly far more than all we can ask or imagine.

Paul ends his glorious doxology in Ephesians 3:20–21 by saying that the glory belongs to God. When God does great things in our lives that we know we could never have done on our own, the glory belongs to God. When the doctors give up on us, but we walk out of the hospital and keep on living as a result of prayer and faith, the glory belongs to God. When people hurt us, lie about us, try to ruin our lives by evil and deception, but God steps in and won't let their evil schemes come to pass, the glory belongs to God.

Then Paul says that the glory also is a result of what God has done in Jesus Christ. I will tell you why I don't mind being "under God" in this world. It is because I know that this life and this world are not all that there is for believers. I know there is a "bright side somewhere."[2] I know there is a land where "the wicked cease from troubling and where the weary are at rest" (Job 3:17). I know that when the earthly house in which I live shall be destroyed, I have another building, a house not made with hands, eternal in the heavens (2 Cor. 5:1).

When I get to the gates of that city I want to be able to speak the right name. I don't want to get up there and say that I could not say the words "under God" because they were unconstitutional. I don't want to have to look at God sitting on the judgment throne in glory and say that I was an atheist and did not believe that God existed. I want to cast my life on the name of him who is able to accomplish abundantly far more than all we can ask or imagine. I want to lift up the name that is above every name. I want to say on that day what the songwriter said,

"Nothing in my hand I bring, simply to the cross I cling."³
And when my feet strike Zion I will not need any prompting to shout and sing:

> *Give glory to God, saints,*
> *Give glory to God.*
> *He's worthy of the praise saints,*
> *Give glory to God.*
> *Sing hallelujah, saints,*
> *Give glory to God.*⁴

I tell you again, being under God is a mighty good place to be!

Notes

Chapter One

1. James Ward and Christine Ward, *Preaching from the Prophets* (Nashville: Abingdon Press, 1995), 11.

2. Adapted from lyrics of "Where Have All the Flowers Gone?" by Pete Seeger, 1955. ©1961 (renewed) Fall River Music Inc. All rights reserved.

3. Ward and Ward, *Preaching from the Prophets*, 11.

4. Warren Stewart, *Interpreting God's Word in Black Preaching* (Valley Forge, Pa.: Judson Press, 1984), 32–33.

5. Martin Luther King Jr., *Letter from Birmingham Jail: Why We Can't Wait* (New York: Signet Books, 1964), 91.

6. Elizabeth Achtemeier, *Preaching from the Minor Prophets* (Grand Rapids: Eerdmans, 1998), 118–19.

7. Walter Brueggemann, *The Prophetic Imagination* (Philadelphia: Fortress Press, 1978).

8. Ibid., 44.

9. Ibid., 30–31.

10. J. Deotis Roberts, *Roots of a Black Future: Family and Church* (Philadelphia: Westminster Press, 1990), 109.

11. Ibid., 110.

12. Abraham Joshua Heschel, *The Prophets* (New York: Harper & Row, 1962), 224.

13. Ibid, 224–25.

Chapter Two

1. John Dart, "Judicial Posts: For Justice or 'Just Us'?" *Christian Century* (May 17, 2005), 14.

2. David D. Kirkpatrick, "DeLay to Be on Christian Telecast on Courts," *New York Times*, August 3, 2005, A15.

3. "Conservatives Mobilizing to Oppose A. G. Gonzales," *The Denver Post*, July 3, 2005, 1A.

4. Dart, "Judicial Posts," 15.

5. Tony Campolo, *Speaking My Mind* (Nashville: W. Publishing Group, 2004), 65.

6. Cynthia Tucker, "Homophobia Rampant in Black America," *Call and Post*, October 24, 2004, A8.

7. Peter Gomes, *The Good Book* (New York: Avon Books, 1996), 144–72, and "Black Christians and Homosexuality: The Pathology of a Permitted Prejudice," *African American Pulpit*, (Summer 2001), 30–33.

8. Ibid., 33.

9. Ibid.

10. "Lack of Black Churches Delays Launch of New Ecumenical Group," *Christian Century* (June 28, 2005), 17.

11. Ibid.

12. William D. Powell, "Baptists' Freedom to Think Is at Risk," *Atlanta Journal and Constitution*, November 24, 2005, A19.

13. Cecil Staton, "Nothing in This Law Will Block Blacks," *Atlanta Journal and Constitution*, November 24, 2005, A19.

14. Martin Luther King Jr., *Letter from Birmingham Jail: Why We Can't Wait* (New York: Signet Books, 1964), 91.

15. Bill McKibben, "The Christian Paradox: How a Faithful Nation Gets Jesus Wrong," *Harper's Magazine* (August 2005), 37.

16. David Briggs, "Lutherans Tackle Issue of Sexuality, Gay Clergy," *The Plain Dealer*, August 8, 2005, A7.

17. Neela Banerjee, "Conservative Episcopalians Warn Church That It Must Change Course or Face Split," *New York Times*, November 12, 2005, A8.

18. David Briggs and Frank Bentayou, "Rulings on Gays Have Some Methodists Struggling," *Plain Dealer*, November 5, 2005, E5.

19. Ibid.

20. "Reformed Church Author OKs Gay Marriage," *Christian Century* (June 28, 2005), 13.

21. "White Ministers Who Took Stand against Racism in '60s Meet in Mississippi," *Jet* (June 20, 2005), 5–6.

22. Barbara Reynolds, "Preachers Would Leave Us at the Back of the Bus," *City News* (February 24–March 2, 2005), 19.

23. Tim Allston, "Black Leaders Discuss Same-Sex Marriage," *Message* (July/August 2005), 24.

24. Marvin A. McMickle, *An Encyclopedia of African American Christian Heritage* (Valley Forge, Pa.: Judson Press: 2001), 10–12.

25. Ibid., 62–64.

26. McKibben, "The Christian Paradox," 32.

27. Ibid.

Chapter Three

1. Charles Colson, "What is Justice?" *Christianity Today* (August 2005), 80.

2. Ibid.

3. John Donne in *The Oxford Dictionary of Quotations*, (New York: Oxford Press, 1966), 186:27.

4. Martin Luther King Jr., *Letter From Birmingham Jail: Why We Can't Wait* (New York: Signet Books 1964), 77.

5. Cleophus LaRue, *The Heart of Black Preaching* (Louisville: Westminster John Knox Press, 2000), 22–23.

6. Jonathan Kozol, *Savage Inequalities* (New York: Harper Perennial, 1991).

7. Marvin A. McMickle, "Social Security: It's a Helping Hand, Not a Stock Market Tool," *Plain Dealer*, August 12, 2005, B10.

8. "Extending Democracy to Ex-Offenders," editorial desk, *New York Times*, Wednesday, June 22, 2005, A18.

9. Gary Fields, "Commission Finds Racial Disparity in Jail Sentencing," *Wall Street Journal*, November 24, 2004, A4.

10. Ibid.

11. Reginald Wilkinson, "They Paid for Their Crime and Need a Second Chance," *Plain Dealer*, June 28, 2005, B9.

12. Ibid.

13. Martin Luther King Jr., "A Time to Break Silence" in *A Testament of Hope: The Essential Writings of Martin Luther King, Jr.*, ed. James Melvin Washington (San Francisco: Harper & Row, 1986), 231–44.

14. James Ward and Christine Ward, *Preaching From the Prophets* (Nashville: Abingdon Press, 1995), 11.

Chapter Four

1. Daniel Ellsberg, "The Posse in the Pulpit," *Time* (May 23, 2005), 32–33.

2. Paul Nowell, "Pastor Calls Ouster of 9 a Misunderstanding," *Plain Dealer*, May 9, 2005, A8.

3. George F. Will, "Brownback's Plans for 2008," *Newsweek* (June 6, 2005), 70.

4. "Worship as Higher Politics," *Christianity Today* (July 2005), 22.

5. Stephen L. Carter, "First Things First," *Christianity Today* (July, 2005), 54.

6. "Rick Warren Publicly Pursuing Programs Against World Poverty," *Christian Century* (July 12, 2005), 15–16.

7. David Brooks, "A Natural Alliance," *New York Times*, May 26, 2005, A29.

8. Ibid.

9. Ibid.

10. Susan Page, "Christian Right's Alliances Bend Political Spectrum," *USA Today*, June 15, 2005, A1.

11. Ibid., A2.

12. OhioRestorationProject.com/plan.php (accessed June 16, 2005).

13. Bill McKibben, "The Christian Paradox: How a Faithful Nation Gets Jesus Wrong," *Harper's Magazine* (August 2005), 32–33.

14. John Lentz, "Drawing the Line between Churches and Politics," *Plain Dealer*, May 31, 2005, B8.

15. "Where's the Compassion," *Christian Century* (March 22, 2005), 5.

16. Elizabeth Bumiller, "Stern Words from the Preacher at the President's Side," *New York Times*, September 19, 2005, A19.

Chapter Five

1. John Leland, "A Church That Packs Them in, 16,000 at a Time," *New York Times*, July 18, 2005, A1.

2. Ibid.

3. Ibid.

4. Ibid.

5. Jason Byasse, "Be Happy: The Health and Wealth Gospel," *Christian Century* (July 12, 2005), 20–21.

6. From "For Every Mountain" by Kurt Carr, released in 1997 on *No One Else*, the Kurt Carr Singers.

7. J. Wendell Mapson, *The Ministry of Music in the Black Church* (Valley Forge, Pa.: Judson Press, 1984), 17.

8. Nick Salvatore, *Singing in a Strange Land: C. L. Franklin, the Black Church, and the Transformation of America* (New York: Little & Brown, 2005), 56.

9. Ibid.

10. Clarence James, "Lost Generation or Left Generation?" quoted in "Preachers Would Leave Us at the Back of the Bus," by Barbara Reynolds, *City News*, February 24–March 2, 2005, 19.

11. Marvin A. McMickle, *Preaching to the Black Middle Class* (Valley Forge, Pa.: Judson Press, 2000), 99–101.

12. Robert McCracken, *The Making of the Sermon* (New York: Harper & Row, 1956.

13. James H. Cone, "The Servant Church," *The Pastor as Servant*, ed. Earl E. Shelp and Ronald H. Sunderland (New York: Pilgrim Press, 1986), 63–64.

Chapter Six

1. John Locke, *Second Treatise on Civil Government*, VII, 87–89.

2. www.revike.org/bio.asp, and "A Prophet's Party? Oh, What a Night!," *Gospel Today* (August 2004), 9.

3. Eddie L. Hyatt, "Have We Misjudged the Word-Faith Movement?" *Ministries Today* (July/August 2005), 36–37; Ted Olsen, "Kenneth Hagin, 'Word of Faith' Preacher, Dies at 86," Christianitytoday.com (September 22, 2003), 1–2; Bill Smith and Carolyn Tuft, "TV Evangelists Call Signals from the Same Play-book," www.trinityfi.org/press/JoyceMeyer4.html, reprinted from "The Prosperity Gospel," *St. Louis Post-Dispatch*, Tuesday, November 18, 2003.

4. Brian Grow, "Church of the Mighty Dollar," Business Weekonline, May 23, 2005, 1.

5. Ibid., 3.

6. Smith and Tuft, "TV Evangelists Call Signals from the Same Playbook."

7. Ibid.

8. "Cheap grace" is a term used by Dietrich Bonhoeffer in *The Cost of Discipleship* that describes a relationship with Christ that costs us nothing. All we have to do is accept forgiveness without responding with lives of discipleship.

9. Smith and Tuft, "TV Evangelists Call Signals from the Same Playbook."

10. Warren Stewart, *Interpreting God's Word in Black Preaching* (Valley Forge, Pa.: Judson Press, 1984), 32–33.

11. James Ward and Christine Ward, *Preaching From the Prophets* (Nashville: Abingdon Press, 1995), 11.

Chapter Seven

1. Cornel West, *Democracy Matters: Winning the Fight against Imperialism* (New York: Penguin Press, 2004), 114–15.

2. Madeleine S. Miller and J. Lane Miller, eds., *Harper's Bible Dictionary* (New York: Harper & Row, 1961), 608–9.

3. Ibid., 609.

4. James Ward and Christine Ward, *Preaching From the Prophets* (Nashville: Abingdon Press, 1995), 11.

5. A term coined by Kenneth Stampp in *The Peculiar Institution* (New York: Knopf, 1956) to define slavery as it was practiced in the United States in the nineteenth century.

6. Paxton Hibben, *Henry Ward Beecher: An American Portrait* (New York: Readers' Club, 1942), 136.

7. "Charles Finney," in *20 Centuries of Great Preaching*, vol. 3, ed. Clyde Fant Jr. and William Pinson Jr. (Waco, Tex.: Word Books, 1971), 320–23.

8. Theodore Parker, "A Sermon on Slavery," in *Sermons in American History*, ed. DeWitte Holland (Nashville: Abingdon Press, 1971), 208–18.

9. Desmond Tutu, *God Has a Dream* (New York: Doubleday Books, 2004), 63.

10. Ibid.

11. Adam Fairclough, *To Redeem the Soul of America: The Southern Christian Leadership Conference and Martin Luther King Jr.* (Athens: University of Georgia Press, 1987).

12. Mark Lewis Taylor, *Religion, Politics, and the Christian Right* (Minneapolis: Fortress Press, 2005, 10–11.

13. West, *Democracy Matters*, 114.

14. "Jarena Lee" in *The Encyclopedia of African American Christian Heritage*, comp. Marvin A. McMickle (Valley Forge, Pa.: Judson Press, 2001), 70–72

15. Ibid., 70–71.

16. Ibid., 10–11.

17. Ibid., 35–36.

18. Beverly Zink-Sawyer, *From Preachers to Suffragists* (Louisville: Westminster John Knox Press, 2003), 2.

19. Ibid.

20. Ibid., 17.

21. Ibid., 7.

22. Joy Ann McDougall, "Women's Work," *Christian Century* (July 26, 2005), 20.

23. Ibid.

24. Demetrius K. Williams, *An End to This Strife: The Politics of Gender in African American Churches* (Minneapolis: Fortress Press, 2004), 71.

25. Ibid.

26. Robert Moats Miller, *Harry Emerson Fosdick: Preacher, Pastor, Prophet* (New York: Oxford Press, 1985), 490–91.

27. Marvin McMickle, "War! What Is It Good For?" *Living Pulpit* (October–December 2005), 16.

28. William Sloane Coffin, *A Passion for the Possible: A Message to U.S. Churches* (Louisville: Westminster John Knox Press, 2004), 19.

29. "God of Grace and God of Glory," lyrics by Harry Emerson Fosdick, *The Worshiping Church: A Hymnal* (Carol Stream, Ill.: Hope Publishing, 1990), 669.

30. West, *Democracy Matters*, 114.

31. Ward and Ward, *Preaching from the Prophets*, 11.

Sermon

1. From the song "I Will Trust in the Lord," arranged by Jeffrey Radford and Nolan Williams, GIA Publications, Inc., 2000.

2. From the song "There's a Bright Side Somewhere," text anonymous, arranged by Joseph Joubert, GIA Publications, Inc. 2000.

3. From the hymn "Rock of Ages" by Augustus M. Toplady, 1740–1778.

4. From the song "Give Glory to God, Saints" by Richard Foy, 1995, Redemption Records.

BIBLIOGRAPHY

Achtemeier, Elizabeth. *Preaching from the Minor Prophets*. Grand Rapids: Eerdmans, 1998.

Allston, Tim. "Black Leaders Discuss Same-Sex Marriage." *Message* (July/August 2005), 22–24.

Briggs, David. "Lutherans Tackle Issue of Sexuality, Gay Clergy." *Plain Dealer*, August 8, 2005, A7.

Briggs, David, and Frank Bentayou. "Rulings on Gays Have Some Methodists Struggling." *Plain Dealer*, November 5, 2005, E5.

Brooks, David. "A Natural Alliance." *New York Times*, May 26, 2005, A29.

Brueggemann, Walter. *The Prophetic Imagination*. Philadelphia: Fortress Press, 1978.

Bumiller, Elizabeth. "Stern Words from the Preacher at the President's Side." *New York Times*, September 19, 2005, A19.

Byasse, Jason. "Be Happy: The Health and Wealth Gospel." *Christian Century* (July 12, 2005), 20–21.

Campolo, Tony. *Speaking My Mind*. Nashville: W. Publishing Group, 2004.

Carter, Stephen L. "First Things First." *Christianity Today* (July, 2005).

Christian Century. "Lack of Black Churches Delays Launch of New Ecumenical Group" (June 28, 2005), 17.

Christian Century. "Reformed Church Author OKs Gay Marriage" (June 28, 2005), 13.

Christian Century. "Where's the Compassion" (March 22, 2005), 5.

Christianity Today. "Worship as Higher Politics" (July 2005), 22.

Coffin, William Sloane. *Once to Every Man and Nation.* New York: Atheneum, 1977.

_____. *A Passion for the Possible.* Louisville: Westminster John Knox Press, 2004.

Colson, Charles. "What is Justice?" *Christianity Today* (August 25, 2005), 80.

Cone, James H. "The Servant Church." *The Pastor as Servant.* Ed. Earl E. Shelp and Ronald H. Sunderland. New York: Pilgrim Press, 1986.

Dart, John. "Judicial Posts: For Justice or 'Just Us'?" *Christian Century* (May 17, 2005).

Denver Post. "Conservatives Mobilizing to Oppose A. G. Gonzales." July 3, 2005, 1A.

Ebony, "The New Black Spirituality" (December 2004).

Ellsberg, Daniel. "The Posse in the Pulpit," *Time* (May 23, 2005), 32–33.

Fairclough, Adam. *To Redeem the Soul of America: The Southern Christian Leadership Conference and Martin Luther King Jr.* Athens: University of Georgia Press, 1987.

Fant, Clyde Jr., and William Pinson Jr., eds. *20 Centuries of Great Preaching.* Vol. 3. Waco, Tex.: Word Books, 1971.

Fields, Gary. "Commission Finds Racial Disparity in Jail Sentencing." *Wall Street Journal,* November 24, 2004, A4.

Fosdick, Harry Emerson. "God of Grace and God of Glory." In *The Worshiping Church.* Carol Stream, Ill.: Hope Publishing, 1990.

Gomes, Peter. "Black Christians and Homosexuality: The Pathology of a Permitted Prejudice." *African American Pulpit* (Summer 2001).

_____. *The Good Book.* New York: Avon Books, 1996.

Gospel Today. "A Prophet's Party? Oh, What a Night!" (August 2004).

Green, Matthew. "Paying the Price." *Ministries Today* (July/August 2005).

Grow, Brian. "Church of the Mighty Dollar." *BusinessWeek online.* May 23, 2005.

Heschel, Abraham Joshua. *The Prophets.* New York: Harper & Row, 1962.

Hibben, Paxton. *Henry Ward Beecher: An American Portrait.* New York: Readers' Club, 1942.

Holland, DeWitte. *Sermons in American History.* Nashville: Abingdon Press, 1971.

Hyatt, Eddie L. "Have We Misjudged the Word-Faith Movement?" *Ministries Today* (July/August 2005).

Ike, Rev. www.revike.org/bio.asp.

James, Clarence. "Lost Generation or Left Generation?" Quoted in Barbara Reynolds, "Preachers Would Leave Us at the Back of the Bus," *City News,* February 24–March 2, 2005.

Jet. "White Ministers Who Took Stand against Racism in '60s Meet in Mississippi" (June 20, 2005), 5–6.

King, Martin Luther, Jr. *Letter From Birmingham Jail: Why We Can't Wait.* New York: Signet Books, 1964.

———. Martin Luther, Jr. "A Time to Break Silence." In *A Testament of Hope: The Essential Writings of Martin Luther King, Jr.* Ed. James Melvin Washington. San Francisco: Harper & Row, 1986, 231–44.

Kirkpatrick, David. "DeLay to Be on Christian Telecast on Courts." *New York Times,* August 3, 2005, A15.

Kozol, Jonathan. *Savage Inequalities.* New York: Harper Perennial, 1991.

LaRue, Cleophus. *The Heart of Black Preaching.* Louisville: Westminster John Knox Press, 2000.

Leland, John. "A Church That Packs Them in, 16,000 at a Time." *New York Times,* July 18, 2005, A1.

Lentz, John. "Drawing the Line between Churches and Politics." *Plain Dealer,* May 31, 2005, B8.

Locke, John. *Second Treatise on Civil Government.*

Mapson, J. Wendell, Jr. *The Ministry of Music in the Black Church.* Valley Forge, Pa.: Judson Press, 1984.

McCracken, Robert. *The Making of the Sermon.* New York: Harper & Row, 1956.

McDougall, Joy Ann. "Women's Work," *Christian Century* (July 26, 2005), 768–70.

McKibben, Bill. "The Christian Paradox: How a Faithful Nation Gets Jesus Wrong." *Harper's Magazine* (August 2005), 32–33.

McMickle, Marvin. *An Encyclopedia of African American Christian Heritage.* Valley Forge, Pa.: Judson Press, 2001.

_____. *Preaching to the Black Middle Class.* Valley Forge, Pa.: Judson Press, 2000.

_____. "Social Security: It's a Helping Hand, Not a Stock Market Tool." *Plain Dealer,* August 12, 2005, B10.

_____. "War! What Is It Good For?" *Living Pulpit* (October–December, 2005).

Miller, Madeleine S., and J. Lane Miller, eds. *Harper's Bible Dictionary.* New York: Harper & Row, 1961.

Miller, Robert Moats. *Harry Emerson Fosdick: Preacher, Pastor, Prophet.* New York: Oxford Press, 1985.

Nowell, Paul. "Pastor Calls Ouster of 9 a Misunderstanding." *Plain Dealer,* May 9, 2005, A8.

OhioRestorationProject.com/plan.php. (Accessed June 16, 2005.)

Olsen, Ted. "Kenneth Hagin, 'Word of Faith' Preacher, Dies at 86," ChristianityToday.com, September 22, 2003.

Oxford Dictionary of Quotations. John Donne. New York: Oxford Press, 1966.

Page, Susan. "Christian Right's Alliances Bend Political Spectrum." *USA Today,* June 15, 2005, A1.

Parker, Theodore. "A Sermon on Slavery," in *Sermons in American History,* Ed. DeWitte Holland. Nashville: Abingdon Press, 1971.

Powell, William D. "Baptists' Freedom to Think Is at Risk." *Atlanta Journal and Constitution,* November 24, 2005, 17.

Reynolds, Barbara. "Preachers Would Leave Us at the Back of the Bus." *City News,* February 24–March 2, 2005, 19.

Roberts, J. Deotis. *Roots of a Black Future: Family and Church.* Philadelphia: Westminster Press, 1990.

Salvatore, Nick. *Singing in a Strange Land: C. L. Franklin, the Black Church, and the Transformation of America.* New York: Little, Brown, 2005.

Smith, Bill, and Carolyn Tuft. "TV Evangelists Call Signals from the Same Playbook." www.org/press/JoyceMeyer4.html. Reprinted from "The Prosperity Gospel." *St. Louis Post-Dispatch,* November 18, 2003.

Staton, Cecil. "Nothing in This Law Will Block Blacks." *Atlanta Journal and Constitution,* November 24, 2005, A19.

Stewart, Warren. *Interpreting God's Word in Black Preaching.* Valley Forge, Pa.: Judson Press, 1984.

Taylor, Mark Lewis. *Religion, Politics, and the Christian Right.* Minneapolis: Fortress Press, 2005.

Tucker, Cynthia, "Homophobia Rampant in Black America," *Call and Post,* October 24, 2004, A8.

Tutu, Desmond. *God Has A Dream.* New York: Doubleday Books, 2004.

Ward, James, and Christine Ward. *Preaching from the Prophets.* Nashville: Abingdon Press, 1995.

Washington, James M., ed. *A Testament of Hope: The Essential Writings of Martin Luther King Jr.* San Francisco: Harper & Row, 1986.

West, Cornel. *Democracy Matters: Winning the Fight against Imperialism.* New York: Penguin Press, 2004.

Wilkinson, Reginald. "They Paid for Their Crime and Need a Second Chance." *Plain Dealer,* June 28, 2005, B9.

Will, George F. "Brownback's Plans for 2008." *Newsweek* (June 6, 2005), 70.

Williams, Demetrius K. *An End to This Strife: The Politics of Gender in African American Churches.* Minneapolis: Fortress Press, 2004.

Zink-Sawyer, Beverly. *From Preachers to Suffragists.* Louisville: Westminster John Knox Press, 2003.

Printed in the USA
CPSIA information can be obtained
at www.ICGtesting.com
LVHW021413200124
769224LV00004B/268

9 780829 818376